MADE to PRAY

Endorsements for

Made to Pray

This book could radically change how you see God, your life, and your ministry. Chris Heinz' insights into prayer will fill your heart with holy anticipation over what God can do in you and through you. Peppered with riveting stories and practical applications, this book provides you with a clear pathway to explore your tailor-made prayer DNA. I believe *Made to Pray* will quickly find itself on your "best prayer books" list.

–Dr. Doug Shaw,
President/CEO of International Students, Inc.,
Author and Speaker on emerging world religions,
global missions, and globalization

Having known Chris for more than a decade, I have watched him mature from a passionate worshiper to a loving husband, tender-hearted father, and now an amazing author. This is a time to not only embrace the next generation but to empower them to do damage to the kingdom of darkness and bring God's light, glory, and transformation to the nations.

–Tommi Femrite,
Author of *Intercessors: Discover Your Prayer Power*
and Founder of GateKeepers International

Most books about prayer yield instant guilt. Filled with clear explanations and biblical insights, *Made to Pray* yields prayer instead—prayer of the rich, real, and personal kind. Read it. Pray it. And find your life transformed.

–Marti Pieper,
Author, Speaker, and Director of Prayer and Publication,
Awe Star Ministries

Chris Heinz has a true passion for prayer. I've watched him energize audiences with his provoking thoughts. You'll be energized, too, if you embrace his teaching.

—Dannah Gresh,
Best-selling Author of *And The Bride Wore White*

Made to Pray is a fresh, biblical guide to developing a satisfying and fruitful prayer life. It's a must-read for the Body of Christ as we seek a much needed prayer awakening in this generation.

—MaryAlice Isleib,
Author of *Effective Fervent Prayer* and *Healing Toxic Emotions*

Can prayer actually be *fun?* In this entertaining, inspiring, and informative book, Chris Heinz helps you understand the way you were wired to talk with God and the many forms these sacred conversations can take. If you have found yourself floundering in prayer—or avoiding prayer altogether—this is the book for you.

—Nate Larkin,
Founder of the Samson Society and Author of
Samson and the Pirate Monks: Calling Men to Authentic Brotherhood

I love assessments, and though I love the "prayer" assessment that comes with *Made to Pray*, there is much more to the book. Over the years I've watched Chris Heinz follow Jesus and grow in maturity and skill. God has put a passion on his heart to see people deepen their prayer life, and has given him a message that will help that passion come true. Chris comes with a servant's heart, as a practitioner of prayer, not just a teacher. God has made you to pray!

—Dan Nold, Lead Pastor,
Calvary Church, State College, PA

Encouraging, humorous, and light-hearted, I highly recommend *Made to Pray*. This book has what I personally look for to impact my walk with the Lord—its author writes what he writes because he's "been there." You'll be glad you took the opportunity to let it impact you too.

–Father Dimitri Sala, OFM,
Author of *The Stained Glass Curtain:
Crossing the Evangelical-Catholic Divide to Find Our Common Heritage*

In this powerful book Chris Heinz issues a passionate challenge for us to become what we were meant to be. It offers inspiration and guidance by calling Christians to recover their voice and experience a prayer life that is enjoyable, effective, and enduring. In *Made to Pray*, Chris shows us the best incentive for prayer, that when we pray, God gets something no one else can give him—God gets us. In other words, we pray not just to get something from God but to give him what he longs for—ourselves.

–Tim Stoner,
Author of *The Paladins* and *The God Who Smokes*

Wow! As I read *Made to Pray*, I laughed, I cried, I wanted to go tell someone, I read some pieces to my wife. I thought…everyone should read this. This book is so good. Everyone will find a point of contact; everyone will summit a new hill.

–Reverend James Welch,
Founder of Summer's Best Two Weeks Christian Sports Camps

Chris Heinz' book on prayer is like drinking a Red Bull for the first time. It will energize you to pray and build momentum in your prayer life. Simple and straight to the point, it's a good read for anyone looking to connect with the Father.

–Jorn Junod,
Lead Pastor of Discovery Road Church,
State College, PA

Prayer is an essential component of our daily walk with Jesus. In his book, *Made To Pray*, Chris shares some realistic steps to accomplish this daily walk with Jesus. Each chapter provides selected scriptural references and stories that will motivate you and create an awareness of what is going on around you.

—Dr. Ellen Taricani, Author of
His Hiding Place and *Worship in Freedom*

The least attended meeting in the church today is the prayer meeting. *Made to Pray* is a solution to this problem. Not only will it make prayer enjoyable, it's a must-read for people who want to see their cities and nations transformed as they remain connected with God 24/7 and understand they are made to pray.

—King Flores,
Founder of the "My City, God's City Movement"
in Paranaque City, Philippines,
a city dedicated to God with daily prayer
at city hall for eight years running

Chris Heinz isn't simply a champion of prayer. *Made to Pray* is the passion of someone I've watched live out this message for almost a decade. This is not just a book, it's a spirit that will impact you!

—George Bakalov,
President, George Bakalov Ministries Intl.

Too much teaching on prayer is made of platitudes, sugar-laden sentiment, or guilt-inducing directives. But not this book. Chris Heinz has given us a language for prayer. This isn't merely a book to be read, but a book to be experienced. I look forward to seeing what it unleashes in the lives of individuals and the church at large!

—Steve Lutz,
Author of *King of the Campus* and
College Ministry in a Post-Christian Culture

Every chapter of *Made to Pray* brought new clarity and freedom to my communication with God. It seems that so many people are handcuffed to imitating another person's prayer life. *Made to Pray* is a key to set people free, releasing them to a prayer life of great power and intimacy.

–Janet Mylin,
Prayer Coordinator for Centre Church,
State College, PA

Whether you're a new Christian or have known the Lord for years, *Made to Pray* will revolutionize your prayer life. Biblically sound teaching presented in a fresh and refreshing way will challenge you to discover a closer walk with God than you dreamed possible.

–Marlene Bagnull,
Author and Director of the Colorado and
Greater Philadelphia Christian Writers Conference

Are you one of the many people who approach God in prayer fearfully or with feelings of inadequacy? If so, this book is for you! These words written by Chris Heinz are God-inspired. I am delighted by the various ways of prayer articulated in this book. I will be sure to share it with my congregation.

–Reverend Sally D. Zelker,
Pastor of Morgenland Union Church,
Orefield, PA

Imagine having the opportunity to commune with Almighty God. Wow, what a blessing! This is the opportunity available every moment through prayer. Unfortunately, far too many Christians do not take advantage of this blessing. *Made to Pray* is a positive encouragement for Christians struggling with developing a meaningful and consistent life of prayer.

–Harold McKenzie,
Senior Pastor of Unity Church of Jesus Christ,
State College, PA

Made to Pray offers a refreshing new perspective that focuses the reader's attention on God, his ability, his promises and his performance! Guilt-free and grace-full, *Made to Pray* brings out the fun in prayer and demonstrates how effortless communicating with our heavenly Father was meant to be.

—Allan Scott,
Worship Leader and Recording Artist,
www.AllanScottMusic.com

Would you admit that too often your prayer life is boring and difficult to endure even though you long for more? Chris Heinz offers personal and insightful solutions for finding your voice with God through his pragmatic explanation of 12 common prayer types. *Made to Pray* will inspire you to thoroughly enjoy prayer in a fresh new way!

—Sherilyn Jameson,
Director of Small Groups, Calvary Church,
State College, PA

Made to Pray offers a fresh new perspective on prayer! You'll find yourself seeking the prayer types that make you unique and effective for the kingdom. Let Chris Heinz help you discover your prayer strengths.

—Vince Smith,
Pastor of State College Christian Church
and Chairman of Haven of Hope Zambia

Have you ever wanted to have a better prayer life, but felt you just weren't "spiritual" enough? If so, read this book. With clear insight and gut-busting humor, Chris Heinz will start you on an exciting journey towards a vibrant prayer life.

Ted Hahs, Chief Intercessor, Harvest Evangelism, Inc.,
www.TransformOurWorld.org

I always thought of myself as a slacker in prayer. I knew the importance of it, but couldn't find a rhythm. But Chris Heinz helped me to identify my sweet spot in prayer! It helped me to throw off the guilt of not praying like other Christians, and instead pray the way God designed me to pray.

Jonathan Weibel, Church Planter

MADE to PRAY

How To Find Your Best Prayer Types

Chris Heinz

WestBow
PRESS
A DIVISION OF THOMAS NELSON

WestBow Press books may be ordered through booksellers or by contacting:
WestBow Press
A Division of Thomas Nelson
1663 Liberty Drive
Bloomington, IN 47403
www.westbowpress.com
1-(866) 928-1240

Cover design and interior images provided by Andy Mylin.

ISBN: 978-1-4497-8831-5 (sc)
ISBN: 978-1-4497-8832-2 (hc)
ISBN: 978-1-4497-8830-8 (e)
Library of Congress Control Number: 2013904524

Printed in the United States of America
WestBow Press rev. date: 06/26/2014

Dedicated to Colette,
the wildest flower I know.

I love you.

Table of Contents

Acknowledgements

My name is on this book, but there are many names behind it. I'd like to thank God for all the experiences in these pages. You've given me a life beyond my dreams and I'm grateful to you. To my beautiful wife and awesome children, thank you for supporting me as I shut myself in my office to pray and write. This book is good, but you're my best fruit.

Thank you, Mom for bringing Jesus into our family. Thank you, Dad for influencing me more than anyone. To my brothers, thank you for letting me write the opening story in Chapter 9. Thank you to the mentors who have shaped me—George, Dan, David, Jonathan, Ron, John, and Jeff. As you can see, I've needed help. Thank you to my men's circle for loving me and impacting me.

Many prayers brought this book from conception to birth to maturity. Thank you to all those who prayed including: my writing prayer team; the prayer group at EnergyCAP, Inc.; Little Jerusalem House of Prayer in Tondo, Philippines; People's Church in Kegalle, Sri Lanka; Myanmar Agape Ministries in Yangon, Myanmar; Mighty Refuge Prayer Mountain in Harkhar, Myanmar; Calvary Church in State College, PA; and my prayer partner.

Thank you to Grace Prep High School, for letting me test content on you. Thanks, Caleb for your insightful work on the prayer assessment. To those who tested the assessment, wrote discussion questions, let me talk out material, or helped in any other way, thank you.

Thank you to Mark Richard, Joan Didion, Anne Lamott, C.S. Lewis, Annie Dillard, and Robert Benson. You don't know me, but your writing has inspired mine.

And finally, to the readers of my weekly email, thank you for walking with me as I sketch and scribble the meditations of my heart.

Author Foreword

A SHOCKING THING HAPPENED THIS PAST Christmas Day.
A few days before Christmas, I began feeling pain in my chest. At first it felt like a pulled muscle, tightness, like a rubber band being asked to stretch beyond its capacity. It was irritating, so I took aspirin and did my best to ignore it. I went to work, did last minute Christmas shopping, attended the Christmas Eve service and had Christmas Day at home.

But it was while watching *The Christmas Story* in the evening, after Ralphie asked for his Red Ryder BB Gun, when I couldn't take the pain anymore. My chest felt like shards of glass were being scraped under my skin. I could only take short, narrow breaths. I went to the Emergency Room.

They did various tests and scans, and finally delivered the diagnosis: I had suffered a pulmonary embolism—a blood clot in my lung. They admitted me to the hospital and said I was going to be there for a few days. It ended up being a week.

At first it wasn't bad. They brought pain medicine every three hours, and I got to fill in my meal choices on the little menu every morning, and I had lots of visitors. Plus the *Titanic* movie marathon was on TV.

During a commercial, a question popped into my mind: *How serious is a pulmonary embolism anyway?*

I pulled out my iPad and did some research:

According to the Centers for Disease Control, 60,000 to 100,000 Americans die every year from blood clotting in a vein. I later learned that my wife's grandmother died from it, as did a friend's brother. And just a few days after my clot, a 29 year-old woman, newly married, who was a bank teller in our town, died from it.

This was serious. I turned off the TV (I knew how *Titanic* ended). I wanted to listen to the rhythm of my life. My life could have been over, but it was not, so now what?

We all have moments like this, when life and death intersect. A family member dies, or a friend and coworker, a friend's spouse. Or we ourselves have a near-death experience or a medical question that gets us fretting. Or the loss of strangers in tragedies like plane crashes and house fires.

But these brushes with death can be gifts to remind us of life's importances.

Have you ever listened to the rhythm of your life when it was in danger of being taken away? How did it sound?

My sound came in three lessons.

In John 15:4-5, Jesus said,

"Remain in me, and I will remain in you. No branch can bear fruit by itself; it must remain in the vine. Neither can you bear fruit unless you remain in me. I am the vine, you are the branches. If a man remains in me and I in him, he will bear much fruit; apart from me you can do nothing."

I understood that rather than being Vice President of Marketing for EnergyCAP, Inc., or an author and speaker, or even a father and husband, my primary work is to remain in Jesus. By remaining in Jesus, I can be the best marketer, minister, father, and husband possible. Why? Because the fruit of remaining in Jesus is first of all, inward fruit.

We like to think of fruit as getting results, getting 'er done. Having all hats and all cattle, so to speak. It's having the work of our hands to show for it. But, says Galatians 5:22-23, "the fruit of the Spirit is love, joy, peace, patience, kindness, goodness, faithfulness, gentleness, and self-control." God says this fruit comes first. It doesn't come overnight. Fruit is grown.

So let's begin with the work of God's hands in us, then let the work of our own hands follow. This inward fruit will yield incredible fruit outwardly. But the converse isn't true. Outward fruit—results and doings—will not necessarily yield incredible fruit inwardly.

Lesson 1: Who you're becoming is more important than what you're doing.

I went on a date one time and made a complete fool of myself. The story is in this book. After my disastrous display, I didn't expect to see her again. As I drove home, I reflected on my behavior. I felt so small. What an idiot I was. I began to talk to the LORD about it, maybe for some consolation. I said something like, "Wow, she's so beautiful, so amazing...and I'm such an idiot."

But God said something so surprising I almost pulled the car over because it caused my eyes to water. He said, "Yes she is... but you're just as amazing." I immediately felt so seen, so held, so loved by God. I remember sitting up straight and high, like my stature was adjusting to the truth that was being spoken.

We got engaged three months later and this August we'll celebrate 13 years together. She's my Colette.

Jesus said, "Remain in me and I will remain in you" because he loves us. He wants to be with us, even if we act like idiots and make messes.

Some things about God's love:

» The Bible says God will never leave you or forsake you. God always keeps his Word. God will not leave you.

» God's love is not based on your own nature or ability or goodness—it's based on His. God is a God who remains, so believe it.

» God loved you as a sinner. He'll love you if you sin today. He'll love you if you sin tomorrow. Your sin does not determine if God loves you and it does not disqualify you for God's love. The Bible says God loved you first.

» If you feel unworthy of God's love, that's not his doing. God's love is essential—remember He loved you first. First in chronology, first in importance.

» God doesn't just love you, he delights in you. Zephaniah 3:17 says, "The LORD your God is with you, he is mighty to save. He will take great delight in you, he will quiet you with his love, he will rejoice over you with singing."

The greatest proof of God's love for you is that he gave his one and only Son, that whoever believes in him would not perish but have everlasting life. (John 3:16)

Sin created a barrier between you and God, but God sent Jesus to remove it. So if you ask Jesus to remove it, he will. You cannot receive the fullness of God's love without Jesus.

Lesson 2: God's love for you is far greater than you can imagine.

So how do you remain in God's love all the days of your life? For one, you pray. I'm convinced that prayer is the root of relationship with God, a means of God's grace, where God pours out his love every day, and where ministry is made. The challenge is to see prayer for what it is. You may need a fresh vision for prayer.

When you pray, God gets something no one else can give

him—God gets you. The goal is to find your voice in prayer among different types of prayer.

When you do:

» You'll find lots of possibilities for prayer.

» You don't have to pray like other people.

» You can find the prayer types that work best for you.

» You can pray your own prayers.

Lesson 3: God wants you to find your voice in the most important conversation of your life.

Doctors still don't know why I got the pulmonary embolism. You might say I'm not out of the woods yet. But none of us are certain what will happen next, are we? So let's live out our days the best we can.

Choose to remain in Christ so you can become who you're supposed to be. Remember, who you're becoming is more important than what you're doing.

Receive as much as God's love as you can bear. God's love for you is far greater than you can imagine.

Let God love you in prayer. God wants you to find your voice in the most important conversation of your life.

May God bless you richly as you read this book. I'm praying he does.

Chris Heinz
June 2014

Introduction: Please Read

What would happen to us and maybe even to our
parishes and our towns and the whole wide world ...
if we prayed the prayer that we have been given?
—Robert Benson, *In Constant Prayer*[1]

I cried unto God with my voice, even unto God
with my voice; and he gave ear unto me.
—Psalm 77:1, KJV

PRAYER MEETINGS ARE FOR OLD ladies. You've always thought
so. But let's say you decide to attend one anyway. You don't
really want to, but you think it'll be good for you, the same way
vegetables were good for you as a kid. You didn't want to eat
them, but they were supposed to be healthy, and you're feeling
malnourished lately.

So on Friday night, you park in the church's gravel lot and
enter the double doors. You pause before you push them open.
What are you thinking? You have other things to do; you want
to turn around and leave. But no, it'd be the same old thing if you
walk away. You want ... no, you *need* something different now.

So you push your way through the old wooden doors—*creak,
creak*—and enter a room that is furnished with a circle of plush

maroon chairs. You sit down on one of them, flashing a nervous smile to people here and there. You stuff your hands in your pockets to keep them from shaking.

Yup, you were right. Prayer meetings *are* for old ladies. Enter Old Lady. She's short and elderly, as crinkled and crumpled as a cupcake wrapper. The wrinkles on her face display the many pages of her story like the stickers on a quarterback's helmet. She has had many victories. Old Lady's hair sweeps into a neat bun like an angel's halo. She's wearing a purple velvet jogging suit with silver sparkles on the sleeves.

When she arrives, she quickly and purposefully sets up her station; it looks like she's ready to work. She carries a Vera Bradley imitation bag that looks better than a Vera Bradley original. She pulls several items from it: a large Bible, a worn notebook, a Bic pen, and a pack of purple tissues. Old Lady has only a few tissues left. She feels comfortable making herself comfortable here. She removes her shoes, revealing tiny, curled feet in flesh-colored stockings. How cute. Old Lady wears stockings under her jogging suit. You kind of want her for your meemaw.

Old Lady doesn't say much, just a soft "bless you" to whomever her eyes meet. But when the prayer begins, things change. She roars like a lion going after her prey. You're terrified. Where did little Old Lady go? And when did the lioness arrive? Someone bring back the velvet cupcake, please!

The walls seem to shake from the force of her prayers. The ceiling will fall from her sheer gravitas. Her prayers are infused with Scripture, fortune cookies with real wisdom inside. She quotes entire Bible passages, not just from the New Testament, but from the Old Testament as well. She thees, thous and verilys all over the place. It's stuff you skim over in your Bible reading plan—Leviticus, Numbers, Isaiah. You're sure that any minute she's going to recite the whole Book.

Old Lady's prayers are soaked in faith, brimming with confident expectation that God will answer. Like a prosecutor giving her closing arguments, she waves her arms and stomps her feet when she prays. Perry Mason may have met his match. Old Lady makes a convincing argument, and obviously, she'll get whatever she wants. But she's not just a prosecutor—she's also God's best friend.

Old Lady prays with the feather-filled comfort that years of experience bring—the joy of talking with someone you know very well and who knows you, and it doesn't matter what you say as long as you're together. But on the other hand, it *does* matter what you say because you know exactly what the other wants to hear. Old Lady knows what God wants to hear.

But you're not like her. When it's your turn to pray, you mumble something, which clanks on the ground as it leaves your lips. This confirms your growing suspicion—your prayers don't reach heaven. Of course, *all* of Old Lady's prayers do. They soar right to God's ears. They would, she's God's best friend. But you're not. It feels like your prayers fall back to earth with a thud. They have as much airtime as a lead balloon.

Why did you come to this meeting? If you wanted to feel bad about your prayer life, you could have stayed home.

Your prayer life is a major disappointment. You try to stay focused, but you can't. You try to stay interested, but you don't. You're bored, which is really wearing you out. And your prayer life is hurting your self-esteem. You should look forward to prayer. Prayer should be the best part of your day. But it's not. Instead of running to prayer, you avoid it like you're walking to your death, which makes you feel guilty. And who wants to feel guilty all the time?

You think of the person you used to date. You were great together in a group, but when you got alone, you had no clue what to say. Where did the intriguing person from the group go? And who was this? So you yawned, claiming how tired you were, and then pretended to fall asleep on the carpet so you wouldn't have to talk. You did this so many times that eventually your always falling asleep became suspicious. Maybe you weren't tired after all. Finally, you broke up.

It's been this way with prayer. At first, God was really exciting, but you got bored.

You made promises and resolutions to pray more. You sat down to pray, but soon you were thinking about the movie from the night before. And what snarky status to post on Facebook. You caught your mind wandering, so you returned to prayer, but then you noticed the door trim was peeling, and oh, when was this doorknob changed?

You coached yourself to fight the good fight, tried to refocus. "Please bless Aunt Betsy and heal her gout ..." But just as you began again, you rewrote the Facebook status in your mind, and because it was so brilliant, you grabbed your smartphone and posted it. You just had to. Then you tried to find your way back to prayer.

But it was too late. You had seen a picture of kittens boxing and the Grand Canyon and what your friends were up to, which got you thinking about your day—dry cleaning, oil change, work. And you needed to e-mail this person back and make sure to meet that person. And you should get to it because not much was going on here. So you abandoned prayer before it really got started.

This is the story of your life. You're not cut out for prayer. So you get up and leave the prayer meeting. Ironically, you—not Old Lady—are the one who goes into retirement.

This story isn't unique. There are more people who struggle with prayer than who don't. The Bible says, "Hope deferred makes the heart sick" (Proverbs 13:12). There are more people with sick hearts than satisfied hearts when it comes to prayer.

That's to say there are more people whose hopes for prayer are higher than the prayer lives they currently lead. Why is this? Are they asking for too much? Are they unsatisfied because they're impossible to please? Or are they responding to something that's inside of them?

Although he was the Son of God, Jesus had a clear vision for prayer. The book of Luke gives a glimpse into Jesus' prayer life. One particular night after he started his public ministry, Jesus was surrounded by a crowd of people. But he went alone up the mountain and spent the whole night in prayer. The next morning, he acted upon the result of his prayer time—he chose twelve from among the multitude to be his close disciples (Luke 6:12).

Luke 9:18 says Jesus prayed in private. Luke 9:28 says that Jesus took three of his disciples—Peter, James, and John—up a mountain in order to pray. And in Luke 11:1, Jesus was praying near his disciples and after he finished, one of them said, "LORD, teach us to pray." This disciple had observed Jesus' vision for prayer and wanted to grow in prayer. Learning to pray begins with a clear vision for prayer.

Unless you have a clear vision for prayer, prayer won't take hold in your life the way it could, like with Jesus. Within your heart is the capacity to know God. God made you in his image (Genesis 1:27), you are his workmanship (Ephesians 2:10), and he placed prayer in your heart. In his classic book about spiritual disciplines, Richard Foster writes, "All who have walked with God have viewed prayer as the main business of their lives."[2] If prayer isn't your main business, perhaps your vision for prayer isn't clear.

But there's time. Like the one disciple, you can ask Jesus to teach you to pray. You can do this now: "LORD Jesus, please teach me to pray. I want to have the same passion for prayer that you did. I want to make prayer the main business of my life. Give me a greater vision for prayer and the practice to accompany it. Thank you. In your name I ask this, amen."

Here are four helpful ways to think about prayer:

Prayer is the root of your relationship with God. The heart of a person's relationship with God is his or her prayer life. Says Foster, "Of all the spiritual disciplines, prayer is the most central because it ushers us into perpetual communion with the Father."[2] Just because you're a Christian doesn't mean you're closely connected with God. Have you ever known a man and woman who were married on paper, but not connected in relationship? They were legally married, but didn't function relationally as married people.

The same can happen with God. You may have already confessed to God your sinfulness and asked Jesus to be your Savior. In that moment, you were justified—made right—in God's eyes. The blood of Jesus bought you for God and you became a child of God. This, like marriage, was a legal transaction, but like marriage, the legal position didn't guarantee intimacy. Intimacy has to be built; intimacy has to grow. Prayer is a primary way to build intimacy with God, which is why prayer is the root of your relationship with him.

Prayer is a means of God's grace. Foster writes, "Prayer is the central avenue God uses to transform us."[3] You can see how important prayer is to spiritual development. If you avoid prayer, you cut yourself off from the central flow that is meant to transform you. God didn't bring you into his kingdom to leave you the same. He loves you as you are, but he has great plans for you, bigger plans than you can imagine. And he didn't save you so you could pine away for a castle in the clouds. Eternal life began the day you started following Jesus; eternal life began on this earth.

So then, prayer is God's chief work in you. God's grace is a combination of his blessing and power. It is God's grace that changes you so you are not the person you once were. You have grown in love and patience and kindness because of God's grace chipping and adding, removing and filling in. And it is God's blessing that has bestowed goodness and gifts upon you so they are too many to count, and if you were able to see them all stacked up, you would be forever overwhelmed. Prayer is a means of God's grace.

Prayer is your loving place. Prayer is God's most consistent place to love you. What you need is not more knowledge of God's love, but more encounters with God's love. You can understand the love of God with your mind, but until you experience God's love with your heart, you won't really comprehend it. Consider the orphan. You can adopt him, give him a home, and everyday tell him you love him. But just because you say it doesn't mean he knows it.

He won't know he's loved until he feels he's loved. Until love captures his heart and kneads its way through, defying firmly-rooted ideas that he deserved to be abandoned or he's unworthy of love. Regardless of how many times you profess love, it's like a banging gong or clanging cymbal until he himself feels loved. And that comes only through experience. Prayer is the encounter with God that enables you to feel loved by him. Prayer is where God loves you.

Prayer is where ministry is made. You see this pattern in the Bible. Jesus prayed before choosing the twelve. Who would these disciples become? The founding members of the Church that became a worldwide, enduring movement. The Apostle Paul went on his first missionary trip as a result of prayer. What difference did Paul make? He wrote most of the New Testament and catalyzed the church planting movement. Jesus and Paul's first ministry was prayer.

While prayer is God's work in you, prayer is your chief work. It's easy to make ministry the chief work, but this is backward.

Instead, prayer is where ministry is made. Until you treat prayer as your main ministry, your activities will only be fractionally as powerful and successful as their potential. You may accomplish much on your own, but what if you're settling for a shadow of what God intends? Your ideas and abilities aren't big enough. Don't promise God to people, but only give them you. Prayer is where ministry is made.

God put prayer in your heart so you would seek him. And by seeking him, you would know him. When you pray, God gets something no one else can give him—God gets you. *You* were made to pray.

The reason so many people are unsatisfied with prayer is because God placed prayer in their hearts. Within each heart is the capacity to know God. The Bible says that God made us in his image (Genesis 1:27) and we are his workmanship (Ephesians 2:10). The creation longs to know its creator. Prayer is the primary means of knowing God. We were made to pray. *You* were made to pray.

When you pray, God gets something no one else can give him—God gets you.

Psalm 77:1 says, "I cried unto God with my voice, even unto God with my voice; and he gave ear unto me" (KJV). King David used the word *voice* when he didn't have to. To say he cried out to God would have been enough, but David included "with my voice."

But what choice had he but to cry out with his voice? It seems like unnecessary information. David is making a point. He also repeated the phrase. "I cried unto God *with my voice*, even unto God *with my voice*" (emphasis added). The result of David crying out to God with his voice is God listening to him. Obviously, God wanted to hear David's voice in prayer. God wants to hear *your* voice in prayer.

Prayer becomes frustrating when you don't pray with your own voice. You're trying to pray with someone else's voice—the person who led you to Christ or your pastor or your parent or maybe Old Lady. But God made you to pray with your own voice, and that's the voice he wants to hear from you.

Prayer isn't supposed to be the hard work. You've avoided prayer because it was hard. But the hard work was already done. The spotless Lamb already went into the hinterland, past the realm of hope and joy. He went into the enemy's camp, past sin and sadness, and he carried you out on his bloodied and matted back.

The angels rejoiced, the Father whooped and hollered. If you're a Christian, you're in Christ without separation. The moment you decided to follow Jesus, you were reconciled to God without apology. So prayer isn't supposed to be the hard work.

Instead, prayer is where God pours out his love every day. Prayer is where God loves you. If you listened to him more, you would hear him saying, "I love you." And you would say, "I know." But God would say, "No, you don't understand. I *really* love you." And you would say, "I *know.*" But again God would say, "You don't get it. I *really, really* love you." And you would get it, and you would blush that the God of the universe, the bright and morning star, has you on his mind so much. And it would change your entire day, hearing how much God loves you.

Prayer is the reward of walking with God, but so often, you treat it like it's a punishment. Just think what God can do in prayer:

» reveal what is to come, either in your life or someone else's

» heal some pain, whether physical, emotional, or spiritual

» enlist you to tear down demonic strongholds

» overwhelm you with his tangible presence

» help someone through your prayers

» counsel you on confusing issues

» tell you what he thinks of you

» give you gifts of his grace

» forgive your sins

» love you

Does that sound like a punishment to you?

Listen, God wants your prayer life to be enjoyable, effective, and enduring. He doesn't want you to dread prayer like you're walking to your death. He wants you to run to it and receive the life that prayer offers. When prayer is God loving you, all at once prayer is better than you can imagine. It's the reunion of a lost child, the wedding of passionate lovers, the healing of a chronic disease. It's the concert of a great musician, the victory of a mighty warrior, the freedom of a forgotten captive. Prayer is the best day you've ever had.

Why shouldn't prayer be enjoyable, effective, and enduring? Why shouldn't prayer be fun, get results, and be irresistible? Your expectations for prayer are far too low. You think you've figured God out, seen all there is to see, pulled back the curtains. You think God's run out of tricks, said all that he has to say, shown you all of his muscles. But God is far better than you can imagine, and because of this, prayer is much better than you can imagine.

You're called to live by prayer, to be content if you don't have anything but God. It's counting prayer as your breath, the oxygen filling your lungs. Take air away and you'll die. Take prayer away and you'll die too. When prayer is as it can be, it will not matter where you live or what you wear or what you eat because prayer will sustain you.

Prayer is energetic and active. It sends fire through your veins and stirs your deepest desires. Prayer puts your dreams to flight and awakens your hidden abilities. Prayer lands you face-to-face with your creator, who shows you things you never knew. Prayer takes you places, has a life of its own. It is, by definition, life-giving.

But you have to find your voice.

When you read the letters of the apostle Paul, you see that he is exceedingly thankful. Time and again, Paul begins his letters with thanksgiving:

» "I thank my God through Jesus Christ for all of you" (Romans 1:8).

» "I always thank God for you" (1 Corinthians 1:4).

» "I have not stopped giving thanks for you, remembering you in my prayers" (Ephesians 1:16).

That's not all. Of the thirteen letters that are normally attributed to Paul, he is thankful in ten of them. But if you read other biblical writers, they don't sound the same.

Instead of thanks, David offers praise:

» "O LORD, our LORD, how majestic is your name in all the earth! You have set your glory above the heavens" (Psalm 8:1).

» "The LORD is my rock, my fortress, and my deliverer; my God is my rock, in whom I take refuge" (Psalm 18:2).

» Praise the LORD, O my soul; all my inmost being, praise his holy name. Praise the LORD, O my soul, and forget not all his benefits" (Psalm 103:1–2).

And instead of offering praise, Joshua prays God's Word. But not Jeremiah. He receives messages from God and delivers them.

Here are four distinct types of prayer: thanksgiving, praise, praying the Bible, and prophetic. Each sounds unique. Each causes a different effect. Each has its own characteristics. And when each person prays his own type of prayer, he gets results. But there are more than four prayer types. This book discusses twelve of them:

- » praise
- » petition
- » intercession
- » prophetic
- » listening
- » fellowship
- » warfare
- » praying the Bible
- » confession
- » thanksgiving
- » tongues
- » agreement

Twelve prayer types. What does this mean for you? It means there are lots of possibilities for prayer. You don't have to pray like other people do. You can discover the prayer types that work best for you. You can pray your own prayers. Rather than droning on in prayer, you can actually enjoy prayer. And when you enjoy prayer, you'll pray more often. And praying more often, you'll grow closer to God. You'll free yourself up to be you. And you'll free others to be themselves. Finding your best prayer types frees you and others to uniquely connect with God.

Your best prayer types form your sweet spot in prayer. In baseball, the sweet spot is the area of the bat that offers the best potential for a big hit. When you hit the ball on the sweet spot, there's a greater chance of hitting the ball out of the park. There's no crack quite like that.

In personality theory, living from your sweet spot means understanding your inborn personality traits and living from them. If you're introverted, you don't fight against it; you use it to your advantage. If you're extroverted, hey, where's the partay?!

And in spiritual gifts, living from your sweet spot is knowing your spiritual-gift mix and serving God through it. You learn to maximize your effectiveness in the church and the world. Your sweet spot, therefore, offers the greatest potential for success.

» When you understand your personality, it's easier to live day to day.

» When you pursue your talents, you gain satisfaction.

» When you discover your spiritual gifts, you find your place of service.

» When you find your callings, you impact the world.

The same goes for prayer. When you find your sweet spot in prayer, you can achieve a prayer life that is enjoyable, effective, and enduring—prayer as it's meant to be. A goal of this book is to help you discover your best prayer types so you can have a prayer life that's enjoyable, effective, and enduring.

But that's not the only goal. Your prayer life isn't just about you and God.

The cross of Christ has a vertical beam because it unites you and God. The cross restores the vertical relationship between you and your maker. But the cross also has a horizontal beam. The cross of Christ also restores others to God. The horizontal beam reminds you that prayer is also about the world. God loves you, but he also loves the world. Your prayer life is not an exclusive love fest between you and God, and it's not just for your spiritual growth. Your prayer life is also for the world.

Your prayer life is your greatest means of changing the world for Christ.

That's good, because your city could use some help. Binge drinking and promiscuity is up among the college students while church attendance is down. The mobile home owners are being pushed out of their mobile home park, and the residents have no place to go. School scandals litter the headlines. The middle class seems content living on maxed-out credit cards whose balances they can't afford. It seems your city is getting worse, not better.

Plus you have no idea how to reach your neighbors for Christ. You want them to know God, but when you try to share your faith, your mouth fills with sand and you can't think straight. In the book of Philemon, Paul says to be active in sharing your faith so you'll understand every good thing you have in Christ.

But suddenly, your mind locks up, and you can't think of a single benefit of God's kingdom. Why in the world are you a Christian anyway? You don't know. And why would your neighbor want to become one? You haven't a clue.

But if God can do wondrous things in prayer for you, he can do wondrous things for them. In prayer, God answers all your questions about ministering to your neighbor:

» *Who*: As you pray for opportunities, God will highlight specific people he wants to draw to himself. These are your neighbors. Prayer alerts you in whom God is at work.

» *Where*: Prayer is where you gain the authority to minister to them. The root of ministry is love. When you bring your neighbors before the Lord, you gain a divine affection for them, and this affection comes with authority.

» *When*: Prayer prepares you for when to minister. When

you pray for opportunities, God will open them up. You won't have to force anything. God will open the door, and you'll know when to walk through it.

» *Why*: Prayer is why you can reach your neighbor. You love your neighbor because God first loved you. Experiencing God's love in prayer stirs your hunger for your neighbor to experience God's love, which draws you into praying for them.

» *How*: Prayer is how timid little you will become God's partner in reaching the world. Prayer empowers you with the tools of heaven, emboldens you with courage, and fills you with God's wisdom. The horizontal beam of the cross is possible because the vertical is in place.

But God cannot answer these questions if you don't talk with him. When you pray, God can give you strategies for reaching your neighbors, and by reaching your neighbors you reach the world. So in order to change the world, first change your prayer life. Pray the prayer types that work best for you. Your prayer life is your greatest means of changing the world for Christ.

This book includes a prayer type per chapter. Each chapter includes:

» a personal story

» a biblical character who prayed that way

» a key Bible verse

» an explanation of how Jesus relates

» a description of each prayer type

These chapters are introductions to the prayer types, not advanced lessons. Much more has been written and taught by others. The chapters are designed to introduce you to each prayer type and help you identify which might work best for you. To learn more, please dig into other sources.

The book works alongside the prayer assessment, which is in the back of this book or at www.MadeToPray.com. After you answer the questions, you'll receive a ranking of the top prayer types according to your responses. As you go through the book, compare the assessment results with your reading. Pay attention to the prayer types you feel drawn to. Have you ever prayed this way? Have you witnessed others praying this way? Would you like to pray this way? The assessment results ought to confirm your experience with the book.

As you read, keep in mind that just because something is new doesn't mean it's wrong. You might learn about prayer types that are completely new to you. They might seem strange at first, and you will initially not want to pursue them. But keep an open mind about them. Do you feel attracted to them? Do you feel repelled? Do you feel repelled because they're new? Are you curious? God wants you to discover the prayer types that work best for you, so be open to how he might come to you as you read.

Another important component in finding your prayer types is your community—the people with whom you pray. Share your assessment results with your prayer partner, small group, or Bible study and see if they agree. Each chapter includes discussion questions. The members of your whole group can find their prayer types together. Read the book, discuss the questions, and share your assessment results.

Or take your entire church or ministry through the process. Find your prayer types together so you can pray in concert every time. Corporate prayer times are sometimes the most quiet, uncomfortable, and powerless moments in a church service. People excuse themselves to the bathroom when they know it's coming. But find your prayer types together and transform your prayer time into a true hour of power. No one will want to leave the room. Not even God.

New believers can also benefit from learning about the prayer types. Give their prayer lives the best start possible—teach them about the varieties of prayer from the beginning. Build up their prayer lives when they're young and these new believers will not depart from them.

In addition to discussion questions, each chapter also includes inspirational quotations to use as conversation starters. They're short enough to share on Twitter, Facebook, or another social network. There is also a list of them in the back of the book, "103 Tweets from *Made to Pray.*"

So you'll do it because you need something different. With a fresh vision for prayer, you open the next chapter, like an old creaky door. And as you do, the thrill of something new runs through your veins, and you suspect you'll never be the same again. You'll become who you are, the person you were made to be, because you were made to pray.

Tweets from this Introduction

> » When you pray, God gets something no one else can give him—God gets you. @CSHeinz

> » Prayer is where God pours out his love every day. Prayer is where God loves you. @CSHeinz

> » Prayer is the reward of walking with God, but so often we treat it like punishment. @CSHeinz

> » When prayer is as it can be, it will not matter where you live, or what you wear, or what you eat because prayer will sustain you. @CSHeinz

> » Finding your best prayer types frees you and others to uniquely connect with God. @CSHeinz

» When you find your sweet spot in prayer, you can have prayer that's enjoyable, effective and enduring—prayer as it's meant to be. @CSHeinz

» Your prayer life is your greatest means of changing the world for Christ. @CSHeinz

» When you pray, you can receive strategies for reaching your neighbors, and by reaching your neighbors, you reach the world. @CSHeinz

Discussion Questions

1. What words describe your prayer life?
2. Have you ever felt threatened or discouraged by someone else's prayer life? Why?
3. How does it make you feel that God wants to hear your voice?
4. On a scale of one to ten how enjoyable is your prayer life?
5. How much effort have you given to improving prayer?
6. Has God ever surprised you in prayer?
7. Are your expectations for prayer too low?
8. How would you like your prayer life to change?
9. How can prayer help you to reach out to your neighbors?
10. As you read the list of prayer types, which ones interest you? Which ones do not? Do you regularly pray in any of them?

1
Prayer of Praise

My personal prayers of praise expressed my feelings,
fears, and hopes, and without fail, God responded daily
by assuring me of his faithfulness and sovereignty.
—Becky Tirabassi,
Let Prayer Change Your Life—Revised[2]

Let everything that has breath praise the LORD.
—Psalm 150:6

Definition of Prayer of Praise: Declaring the truth about who God
is, what he has done, or what he has promised to do

Bible Character: Peter

YOU DON'T KNOW WHEN YOU'LL return to this part of the
world, so you walk the streets near your hotel. You watch
the people, take in the smells. It's so different from home. Water

has finally receded from the rain. The wet ground is starting to dry. You missed the storm by just days. You wonder how they'll recover. It seems unfair that so many storms have come.

Different colored trash litters the ground; your eyes are drawn to it. There's green glass and brown glass and blue glass. There are sheets of tin and wet cardboard, loose paper strewn about. Shoeless and dirty children waddle around. They pick out trash as toys. They find a tire, roll it to each other and laugh. You can't decide to smile or cry.

What's that on the ground? A piece of paper with writing on it. You notice it among the garbage. You pick up the fragment, mud-stamped and still damp. You can make out the words written in pencil, trampled by little feet:

> God, I praise you in the sun and storm. I praise you in the good times and bad. I praise you for the typhoon. Homes are gone. Much is lost. I don't know what's next. We had little, and now we have less. But I praise you, God. You're the Good Shepherd. We have Jesus and the Holy Spirit. We have all we need! The mud will become dust, but my praise will remain.

What is praise? Well, it's more than music. Praise is more than music and instruments and singing. When you limit praise to music, you perfect the music but forget the point of praise. To praise is to declare the truth about:

» who God is (his identity)

» what God has done (his deeds)

» what God said he will do (his promises)

You can do this with or without music. Unfortunately, much of today's praise music is more about you than about God.

In God, these three areas—his identity, deeds, and promises—always agree with each other. This is to say that God has integrity, which means a wholeness of being. He behaves from his being. He conforms to his character. God's deeds match his identity, which match his promises. Praise the God who is one!

One way to praise is to declare who God is. In Matthew 6, Jesus was praying while his disciples waited for him to finish. When he was done, the disciples asked Jesus to teach them to pray. This is the posture of a disciple. Jesus will teach you to pray when you ask him.

In teaching them, Jesus modeled a prayer to them. It's become known as the Lord's Prayer. He started off, "Our Father in heaven, hallowed be your name." Hallowed means "holy or sacred."[3] Jesus was saying, "God, in the entire universe, there is no one like you. You're different and set apart. You're special." This is a statement of praise. Jesus began his demonstration of prayer with praise. He focused on who God is.

Another way to praise is to declare what God has done. You name the deeds of God. You tell God that you've noticed. So what has God done for you? Praise answers this question.

Truth is, God is at work more than you know. What you need is not for God to do more, but for you to see more of what God has already done. In Psalm 126:3, the Israelites sang, "The LORD has done great things for us, and we are filled with joy." Praise opens your eyes to God's work and fills you with joy.

Praise is also declaring what God has said he'll do; it's proclaiming God's promises. How many promises are in the Bible? Scholars have said three thousand promises, some scholars seven thousand, and still others have said eight thousand. It is difficult to count all the promises in the Bible because there are so many. This is bad news if God doesn't keep his promises. Then the Bible would be filled with broken promises. But it's not. The good news is that God always keeps his promises!

When God says he'll do something, it's as good as done. You can praise him for it now. This is what faith is. Faith is not based on what has already happened, but on what you do not see. Hebrews 11:1 says, "Faith is the assurance of things hoped for and the conviction of things not seen."

So for example, when God says in Hebrews 13:5, "Never will I leave you; never will I forsake you," what does that mean for you? It doesn't take a doctorate in biblical exegesis to interpret this, and yet many people struggle with this promise. Here's what it means. Ready … wait for it, wait for it … now go. This verse means that God will never leave you or forsake you. His presence in your life is certain.

Regardless of who did what to you or what you did knowingly or unknowingly or what is falling apart, God will never leave you. If you really believed this, how would it change your life? God is looking for people who will stand on his promises regardless of what they do not see. This is living by faith. Praise is your agreement with God's promises; it's your "amen" that echoes every one of them.

Now that you know what praise is, what are its benefits?

Praise changes the spiritual climate. Let's say you're walking into a grocery store at Christmastime. The Salvation Army bell ringers are ringing and dinging at the door. But their presentation is amplified—they have a speaker and microphone. They rotate between singing Christmas carols and wishing the listeners a merry Christmas.

The problem is, there's no audience. No one has stopped to listen. They seem to be speaking to the air. But they keep at it. Why? Because they're creating an atmosphere. This is what praise does.

Acts 16 says that Paul and Silas were arrested for preaching about Jesus. They were severely beaten with rods and then put into prison. But this didn't get them down. About midnight, they began praising God while the other prisoners listened. They changed the spiritual climate. Then an earthquake shook and freed Paul and Silas. What could have been a downer turned into deliverance. When you're in a bad mood, begin praising God.

Praise also *fulfills your primary purpose as a created being.* It is primal for creation to praise the Creator. If you don't, you'll worship something else. John 4:23 says, "An hour is coming, and now is, when the true worshippers will worship the Father in spirit and truth; for such people the Father seeks to be his worshippers." God the Father is seeking worshippers.

One day after Jesus performed some miracles, the crowd began praising God. But the religious teachers—the Pharisees—didn't like it. They asked Jesus to rebuke the crowd for praising God. But Jesus said to them, "If these [people] become silent, the stones will cry out!" (Luke 19:40). One of the enemies of praise is religion. Religion is the rote adherence to rules and customs instead of living from a vibrant relationship with God. The quickest way to stifle praise is to be religious. This is why your heart abandoned to God—and not perfect music—is the root of real worship. God prefers passion over form.

Another benefit is that *praise empowers you to great deeds.* In Matthew 16:13, Jesus asked his disciples, "Who do people say the Son of Man is?" They returned a variety of responses—John the Baptist, Elijah, Jeremiah. But none of the people were right, as Jesus wasn't any of them.

Then Jesus asked, "But what about you? Who do you say that I am?" (Matthew 16:15)

It seems like an easy question. This is sixteen chapters into the book of Matthew. The disciples have been through a lot with

Jesus already—the Sermon on the Mount, healings, deliverances, raisings of the dead, teachings, the feeding of the five thousand, walking on water, calming a storm, the feeding of the four thousand, and interactions with religious leaders. It seems like any one of the disciples should have been able to answer it.

But only Simon answered. "You are the Christ, the Son of the living God" (Matthew 16:16). Bingo.

And Jesus said, "Blessed are you, Simon son of Jonah, for this was not revealed to you by man, but by my Father in heaven. And I tell you that you are Peter, and on this rock I will build my church" (Matthew 16:17–18).

Jesus changed Simon's name to Peter. Scholars have suggested that Simon means "reed," while Peter means "rock." In an instant, Jesus began referring to the former reed as the present rock. Why? Because Simon correctly named Jesus for who he was—the Son of God. This is the foundation of the church. This affirmation activates the church to be the people of God. Only through Jesus can Simon attain his destiny. Only through Jesus can the real Peter emerge.

Praise empowered Peter to perform great deeds, and it does the same for you. Consider six things Peter did (and there are many more) after he identified Jesus as the Son of God. You can do the same.

» **Preach the gospel**: "Then Peter stood up with the Eleven, raised his voice and addressed the crowd" (Acts 2:14). Praise empowers you to preach the gospel of Jesus. What else is the gospel but the truth of God?

» **Heal the sick**: "Taking him by the right hand, [Peter and John] helped him up, and instantly the man's feet became strong" (Acts 3:7). Praise reminds you that God heals.

» **Baptize in the name of Jesus**: "So [Peter] ordered

that they be baptized in the name of Jesus Christ" (Acts 10:48). Praise anoints you to make new believers and baptize them.

» **Baptize in the Holy Spirit**: "When [Peter and John] arrived, they prayed for them that they might receive the Holy Spirit" (Acts 8:15–16). Praise entices the Holy Spirit to visit in abundance.

» **Cast out demons**: "Crowds gathered also from the towns around Jerusalem, bringing their sick and those tormented by evil spirits, and all of them were healed" (Acts 5:16). Praise deputizes you to cast out demons.

» **Put on courage**: "When they saw the courage of Peter and John and realized that they were unschooled, ordinary men, they were astonished and they took note that these men had been with Jesus" (Acts 4:13). Praise emboldens you to walk in faith.

In addition to empowering you, *praise reminds you of God's presence in your life*. King David is admired for being a man after God's own heart. His psalms speak of passion and intimacy with God. If there was anyone who was close with God, it was David.

But in Psalm 22:1, David wrote, "My God, my God, why have you forsaken me?" David felt like God had gone. He doubted God's presence in his life. But what is the promise? "I will never leave you or forsake you." If you begin walking with God, be assured—he's close. God wants to be closer to you than you want to be with him. Praise reminds you that God is near.

Praise also crucifies your pride. Do you tend to think of yourself more highly than you ought? Praise humbles you because praise is a sacrifice, and sacrifice always costs you. King David conquered Jerusalem, which was a very difficult city to win. His first act was to bring the ark of the covenant into the city. The ark was the closest thing to the actual presence of God. With musical instruments and singing, all the people rejoiced.

But the level of worship—the status quo of praise—was not enough to express David's heart, so he went further. He stripped down and danced before the Lord, in the sight of all the people. His wife Michal watched from the window and became angry. Second Samuel 6:16 says that she despised him.

In *Listening to Your Life*, Frederick Buechner writes,

> How they cut loose together, David and Yahweh, whirling around before the ark in such a passion that they caught fire from each other and blazed up in a single flame of such magnificence that not even the dressing-down David got from Michal afterwards could dim the glory of it.[4]

This was sacrificial praise because it cost David his dignity. Buechner goes on,

> [David] had feet of clay like the rest of us if not more so—self-serving and deceitful, lustful and vain—but on the basis of that dance alone, you can see why it was David more than anybody else that Israel lost her heart to and why, when Jesus of Nazareth came riding into Jerusalem on his flea-bitten mule a thousand years later, it was as the Son of David that they hailed him.

Sacrificial praise is an act of surrendering your own image, reputation, and self-preservation. It's the statement that you honor God more than appearing respectable or civilized, and it hammers a nail into your pride. Is God more worthy to be worshipped than yourself? Praise says yes.

Your sacrificial praise is one of the only things you can offer God that is truly your own. Your heart is free to choose the object of your worship. And not only that, you decide to which degree you engage your heart in praise. When you worship God sacrificially, you adore God with your freedom. Others might get angry or jealous at such affection, but who cares?

Not only does praise humble you, *praise attracts God's presence.* King Solomon—David's son—led the building of the temple in Jerusalem. When it was finished, the ark that David had brought to Jerusalem was brought into the holy place. Then all the heads of the households and the priests praised God through song and trumpet. There were 120 priests on the trumpet! As a result, God's glory came so strong that "the priests could not stand to minister because of the cloud, for the glory of the LORD filled the house of God" (2 Chronicles 5:14).

But that's not all. Solomon prayed and dedicated the temple to God, praising God by saying, "O LORD, the God of Israel, there is no god like You in heaven or on earth, keeping covenant and showing loving-kindness to Your servants." When Solomon finished, fire streamed down from heaven and consumed their offerings and sacrifices. And again, the glory of the Lord filled the house so that "the priests could not enter the house of the LORD because the glory of the LORD filled the LORD's house" (2 Chronicles 7:2).

Do you see what happens in praise? God is drawn to where he is welcomed. The temple was God's house, but not until they sacrificed and praised did God's glory come. God answers sacrifice, and he inhabits praise. He visits altars established to him. Even in God's house, there is a fuller level of his visitation available. If you want God's glory, praise him!

Praise has different effects on God and Satan. Praise invites God, but praise causes the enemy to run. In the beginning, Satan was created as an angel, a servant of God (read more in the chapter on spiritual warfare). But he didn't want to serve God; he wanted to *be* served. So Satan started a rebellion and took a third of the angels with him. Therefore, the kingdom of darkness is based on rebellion. But praise is based on submission to God.

That's why *praise causes the enemy to flee.* The praise of God is something the enemy hates because he wants to be praised. He wants the glory, the admiration, and the adoration. As many people as he can pull from praising of God, the better for him.

So the devil tempts people to obsess about creating perfect and professional music instead of connecting their hearts to God. He shifts the focus of praise from God to you. He gets you to think you deserve to be comfortable in worship rather than offer sacrificial praise. He makes you think praise is only for the church service. But the truth is, praise is a weapon against the enemy, so use it! If you contain praise to the hour or two that you're in church, you'll miss out on God.

Praise builds intimacy with God. When you focus on who God is, what he has done, or what he has promised to do, you get to know him better. You draw into God's presence. And the more you draw into God's presence, the more you experience him. You learn he is more loving than you thought, more passionate than you dreamed, and more committed than ever. This increases intimacy with him.

What else is intimacy than a deep connection built on experiences together? Praise creates experiences with God. You can't really know God unless you experience him. It's the difference between knowing about God and knowing him personally. Many have turned from God without ever having experienced him. They experienced a critical church or a judgmental Christian, and they thought that's the way God is. But they never experienced God himself. How tragic!

If you want to know God, praise him! Praise opens the door to intimacy with God that you thought was only for other people. But it's not. Listen; if you're in Christ, you're already seated at the right hand of God. You're already in the heavenly place. So lean over and sit with God awhile. He wants to sit with you forever.

Praise becomes a testimony for others. The root of the word for *testimony* is "to do again." When you share with others who God is, what God has done, or what he has promised, it becomes a testimony. They might be standing in a place of fear or doubt, but your testimony can restore belief or trust. They might need to hear what God has done in your life, because if he did it for you, he can do it for them. Your belief can spur their belief.

Revelation 12:11 says, "And they overcame because of the blood of the Lamb, and because of their testimony, and they did not love their life even faced with death" (NASB). Let God's people be a people of testimony. God is always at work around and among you. Call him out when you see him. Name the marvelous riches of the Lord. Remind others what he has promised. When God does something for you, share it! Your testimony is a seed of praise that spurs faith in others when they don't have any.

Praise restores your understanding to the right order. When things go wrong, they take control. The broken water softener gets the upper hand. The prodigal son becomes your obsession. But in reality, God is still on the throne. Praise puts things in the right perspective.

When you got married, you had plans for a big family. Now your wife is pregnant—this is going to be easy! Nine months later you have a baby daughter.

But the next kid takes longer, years. What's wrong with you? You meet with a fertility specialist. After a series of tests, she comes back with her diagnosis—there's nothing wrong with either of you. The doctor calls it "unexplained infertility."

Unexplained infertility? What are you supposed to do with that? There's no clear problem to solve, and with no clear problem to solve, there's no way to fix it. And with no way to fix it, you have nothing to do. You feel useless.

Your friends are having babies left and right. They don't mean to conceive, but oh, it happened again. Teenagers are getting pregnant; delinquents are becoming parents. Why can't you have a baby? You're not getting any younger. You feel hopeless.

Then you read Psalm 68:5–6, "God is a Father to the fatherless and sets the lonely in families." You walk outside and look into the night. You see the stars shining like bits of glass in the sky. Every star had its own beginning. Every star has its current place. God planned them all. Maybe God is the cause of your unexplained infertility!

What? How could that be? Because God always behaves from his being. God is the Father of the fatherless.

Now you understand what's happening to you. All this time you thought something was wrong with you. But it had less to do with you and more to do with God. So you begin the process that takes more years. But one day you travel to the distant place.

The phone in your hotel room rings. They're ready for you. He's ready for you. He is why you've come this far.

Normally, he would be playing in the trash, roping the tire, dodging the glass. Napping in the street, peeing in the puddle, running from robbers. He'd be scavenging for leftovers behind the stores and restaurants. And he'd be wanting to be rocked to sleep in soft, firm arms and fall asleep with his head leaning on a beating heart and a lullaby in his sweet ears. He's why you've come to the Philippines.

And when you meet him, big bright eyes like fantastic stars, you praise the God who puts the lonely into families. He cares enough to shut the wombs of certain mothers. God saw that this boy needed a family, and your family would, in time, understand what you were to do. You'd stretch and scramble a bit, but as unthinkable as it was, you would come to praise the God who shuts wombs. Praise the Father of the fatherless. And from your soul bellows a most sincere praise,

> Praise the Father of the fatherless, who shuts wombs but opens families. Praise the God of wonders, who wonders with his love and marvels with his purposes. Who can fathom your plans, O Lord? Your eyes are on the orphan, your heart is on the least of them, and your hands are on my family. I praise you for increasing my family in a most unexpected way.

And that night, your boy is rocked to sleep with a song, head to beating heart. He sleeps soundly with no fear of danger, like a child should. And the next day, you bury your prayer in the dirt. You will leave this land, but your praise will remain.

TWEETS FROM THIS CHAPTER

» When you limit praise to music, you perfect the music, but forget the point. Praise is about God, his deeds, and his promises. @CSHeinz

» Your heart abandoned to God—and not perfect music—is the root of real worship. God prefers passion over form. @CSHeinz

» God is at work more than you know. What you need is not for God to do more, but for you to see more of what God has already done. @CSHeinz

» God is looking for people who will stand on his promises

regardless of what they do not see. This is living by faith. @CSHeinz

» Praise is meant to be a sacrifice and is one of the only things you offer God that is truly your own. It is borne of your freedom. @CSHeinz

» If you want God's glory, then praise him. He visits altars established to him and answers sacrifices offered to him. @CSHeinz

» A strategy of the enemy in worship is to shift the focus from God to you. You'll think you deserve to be comfortable in praise. @CSHeinz

» When God does something for you, share it! Your testimony is a seed of praise that spurs faith in others when they don't have any. @CSHeinz

» When things go wrong, they take control. But in reality, God's still on the throne. Praise puts things in the right perspective. @CSHeinz

Discussion Questions

1. What is the definition of praise?
2. When have you praised God in good times? Difficult times?
3. Was there a difference in how you praised God in both those times?
4. Do you feel you know God well enough to affirm him with praise?
5. How can you get to know God more deeply and intimately?
6. Which three character traits of God stand out to you? How did you learn them?

7. How has praising God changed you?

8. Which benefits of praise could you use right now?

9. What will you do to share God stories that can become seeds of praise for others?

10. Do you feel drawn to this prayer type?

2
Petition Prayer

The right way to approach God is to stretch out your hands
and ask of one who we know has the heart of a Father.
—Dietrich Bonhoeffer, *The Cost of Discipleship*[5]

So I say to you: Ask and it will be given to you; seek and
you will find; knock and the door will be opened to you.
—Luke 11:9

Definition of Petition Prayer: Seeing a need and praying for it

Bible Characters: The leper and the centurion (Matthew 8)

OU HEAD INTO THE GROCERY store and grab for a cart, but a
lady with a young kid is in front of you. She's trying to get
him to sit in the cart, but he won't. The kid kicks and squirms as
the mother struggles to place him inside. He doesn't like the cart,
and this is slowing you down.

She drops her coupons, and they scatter on the floor. She puts the boy down to collect her coupons, but he runs from her and is soon out of reach. She chases the boy, leaving the papers on the ground. You sigh, this is not what you need right now. You step over the coupons, get a cart, and find your aisle.

A few minutes later, you hear the boy in another aisle. His fussing is getting louder. You turn and here he comes, in the cart but trying to climb out. The mother is trying to keep him in. How annoying. Can't you shop in peace?

After a few more aisles, you finish your list. You walk toward the checkout and see the lady and her son again, but not before you hear him. He's still carrying on. And ugh, you'll have to pass them to get out. What a day.

But someone is talking with them, a man. It doesn't seem like they know each other.

As you walk by, you hear the man say, "It looks like you could use some prayer. Mind if I pray for you?"

The mother clears her throat and says, "Umm … sure. Just make it quick."

The man prays to God, asking for strength and rest. "It must be hard being a mom," he prays. And he asks God to encourage her.

"I think he just did," she says as a tear trickles down her face.

This reminds you of a certain friend. She prays for people all the time, doesn't matter where she is. She prays for strangers— people on the sidewalk, in restaurants, at the bank. They don't ask for it, but *boom*, she calls down heaven on their behalf. And she prays for the impossible, things you would never dare ask for. She's so wild. You want to be like her.

But how could you? She's always got stories of this prayer and that. The last time she went on vacation, she prayed for the family of a blind girl, right on the pool deck. "I know God heals blind people," she told the mother. "In fact, I believe today God healed someone who was blind. He can do it for your daughter." So in front of the sunbathers and the well-oiled seniors and the polka-dotted bikinis, she asked God to open heaven.

"Did he heal her?" you ask.

"Not then," she answered. "But it doesn't mean he won't."

And she concluded, "I've learned to ask God for what I'd like him to do. That's the key to miracles on the pool deck. If I ask, they might happen, but if I don't, they won't."

Petition prayer is seeing a need and praying for it. It's based on the words of Jesus, "Ask and it will be given to you; seek and you will find; knock and the door will be opened to you" (Luke 11:9).

There are four secrets to asking God for something. In Matthew 8, Jesus was teaching from the mountainside. When he finished, large crowds followed him, including a man with leprosy. The leper knelt before him and said, "Lord, if you are willing, you can make me clean" (Matthew 8:2).

So Jesus reached out his hand, touched the man, and said, "I am willing, be clean!" And with that, his leprosy faded away.

Next, Jesus went to Capernaum. A centurion approached him and said, "Lord, my servant lies at home paralyzed and in terrible suffering." Jesus agreed to go and heal him. But the centurion replied, "Lord, I do not deserve to have you come under my roof. But just say the word, and my servant will be healed" (Matthew 8:8).

And the servant was healed right then.

The first secret to asking God for something is to just do it. You don't get if you don't ask. The leper and centurion did. This was petition prayer. Notice the leper asked something for himself. It's alright to ask God to move on your behalf. You don't have to spend all your time praying for others. The secret is to just do it. Knock and the door will be opened to you, Jesus said (Luke 11:19).

Jesus invites you to ask. Something stirs your heart—it's justice or mercy or love. The centurion didn't want his servant to suffer; your friend desired more for the family. Or perhaps it is desperation. The leper grew tired of his illness. He had no solutions on his own.

In order for you to ask for God to fill a need, you have to see a need. You have to pay attention to the world around you. Much of life is lost to you because you stick on your headphones and close your eyes to your surroundings. You have to get to where you're going, there's no margin for extra. But that's where miracles happen most, at the unplanned edge. Petition prayer happens when you engage the world around you.

The second secret of petition prayer is to ask boldly. In the passage when Jesus invites you to ask, he tells a story. He says to imagine that you have a friend who comes to your house at midnight. You have finally put your kids to sleep and have gone to bed yourself. But your friend knocks on your door at midnight, saying, "Friend, I need some food because another friend of mine showed up at my house and I have nothing to give him to eat. My pantry is empty."

And you say, "Don't bother me. Everyone's already asleep, and I have an early morning. Go away."

But despite the lateness of the hour, you give your friend all the food he wants, not because he's your friend, but because he's so bold.

So don't just ask—ask boldly. Jesus dares you to.

But what gives you the right to be so bold?

Sometimes desperation moves you to boldness. You have no solution but for God to show up and do something. You need him to. Your suffering is too great. Your ingenuity has run out. Your creativity has dried up. Your magic is gone. Your strength is no more. You have no other choice. You can't get out of this on your own.

Or sometimes your position in Christ moves you to boldness. Ephesians 2:6 says, "And God raised us up with Christ and placed us with him in the heavenly realms." Where are you seated now? With Christ in the heavenly realms. Your body may be on earth, but your position is with Christ. Which is easier? To ask God from Earth where you have to shoot through the atmosphere to a different realm? Or to ask God from heaven where you're seated with Christ at God's right hand?

Sometimes partnership with God moves you to boldness. Ephesians 2:10 says, "For we are God's workmanship, created in Christ Jesus to do good works, which God prepared in advance for us to do." You were created to do good works. But not only that, you are God's fellow worker. He calls you his building (1 Corinthians 3:9). So as God's partner, filled with callings, gifts, talents, and experiences, you can ask boldly so you can accomplish what he set you here to do. Annie Dillard wrote, "There is something you find interesting, for a reason hard to explain. It is hard to explain because you have never read it on any page; there you begin. You were made and set here to give voice to this, your own astonishment."[6] Give flight to your good works, God's fellow.

Or sometimes sonship moves you to boldness. Romans 8:15 says, "For you did not receive a spirit that makes you a slave again to fear, but you received the Spirit of sonship. And by him we cry, 'Abba, Father.'"

Being in Christ makes you a son or daughter of God. You can ask, knowing God is your perfect Father who is working for your good. He's patient, compassionate, and loving beyond measure. God won't slap you when you draw near. He'll pull you into his strong, loving arms, which are iron and velvet at once.

Wow, you suddenly realize how little you have knocked, how

little you have asked for. You thought God found your requests annoying. You thought he laughed at your desires.

But he didn't.

God is daring you to ask for great and many things that will cause people to gasp when they happen and say, "Surely God is here."

The third secret is to ask in faith. Faith is a root of the Christian life. To ask in faith is to ask of God. Asking in faith means to ask for the impossible. Why? Because "with God nothing is impossible" (Luke 1:37). A problem in prayer is asking for what you already have, what you can do on your own, or what you already see. This isn't faith; it's asking by sight. "Now faith is being sure of what we hope for and certain of what we do not see" (Hebrews 11:1). To ask in faith is to ask for what you don't presently see, possess, or can do independently.

When you pray for the impossible, God's ability to do the impossible is based on his character, not your perfect prayer, behavior, or understanding. E. M. Bounds wrote, "God put no limitation on his ability to save through true praying. The possibilities of prayer are linked to the infinite righteousness and to the omnipotent power of God. There is nothing too hard for God to do."[7] So when you ask in faith, ask the one who is able to do it.

The fourth secret is to submit to God's will. Once there was a mother who loved her boy very much. One day, the amount of her love overwhelmed her, and she felt she would burst if she didn't express her love. She said, "Son, I love you so much that I'll give you anything you want."

"You will? Then I'd like to eat French fries every day of my life."

"You'd like to eat French fries every day of your life?" she asked.

"Yes, and I'd like to drown them in ketchup too."

"I see," the mom said.

The mom now had a dilemma. She could answer her son's request, but it wouldn't be best for him to eat French fries and ketchup every day of his life. Or she could deny her son's request, but he might get upset with her and doubt her love because she didn't give him what he asked for.

So she said, "Son, you can always ask me for what you want, but I have a question for you. Is it best for you to eat French fries and ketchup every day of your life? Or is it best for you to trust me?"

"It's best for me to trust you," the boy said.

In the garden of Gethsemane, Jesus was deciding whether or not to go the cross. He fell with his face to the ground and prayed, "My Father, if it is possible, may this cup be taken from me. Yet not as I will, but as you will" (Matthew 26:39).

Jesus knew the horrors that faced him at the cross, so he asked for a way out.

But he trusted God anyway and submitted his desire to the will of God. His prayer basically was, "I don't want to do this, but if you want me to, I will."

The leper said, "If you are willing, you can make me clean" (Matthew 8:2). God healed the leper.

The centurion said, "Just say the word, and my servant will be healed" (Matthew 8:8). God healed the servant.

Jesus said, "I don't want to do this, but if you want me to, I will." God sent Jesus to the cross.

Why? Romans 8:28 says, "And we know that in all things God works for the good of those who love him, who have been called according to his purpose." God even works through unanswered prayer. Learn to ask for what you want God to do, but submit to his will when you do.

So let's say you want to start praying for people who didn't ask for it. The first question is, should you? Is it appropriate to pray for strangers in public? Or should you wait for the prayer line at church or your Bible study or for a coworker to ask you to pray?

In Luke 10, Jesus gathered seventy-two disciples and sent them out in pairs into the neighboring towns. Their mission was to pray for people. When God moved as a result of their prayers, they were to tell them the kingdom of God was near. In short, they were to preach the gospel through prayer. This is a mission of the church.

When the seventy-two did this, they were amazed at the results. They returned to Jesus with joy. This in turn filled Jesus with great joy and he praised God (Luke 10:21). Do you want to fill Jesus with joy? Then try this. When you pray for strangers, try to SEE:

> » S—See. Identify someone you want God to touch.

> » E—Engage. Step out and make contact.

> » E—Encounter. Facilitate an encounter with the Father's love.

Identify someone you want God to touch, See. For the seventy-two, it was the people in the towns where they were sent. For you, it might be someone at the mall. Let's say you're at the mall. Rather than making your list and going about your business, you stop to pray first. You ask God to make you sensitive to the needs around you so you can be Jesus at the mall. This changes your perspective. Rather than going, you feel sent.

You do need to find something orange, so you head to a department store first. A salesperson asks if you need help, and you say yes. She finds some stuff, and after trying the clothes on, you're ready to buy them.

Step out and make contact, Engage. This is the hardest step because it initiates movement and requires risk. As the salesperson runs the cash register, you talk, and as you talk, you feel the urge to pray for her. You ask her if you can, and she agrees. You don't make it a big show. You're casual and laid back and speak in words she can understand.

When you pray for her, you keep your voice at conversation level not to embarrass her. She continues to ring up your items as you pray.

Facilitate an encounter with the Father's love, Encounter. The salesperson might have a pressing need. A physical or emotional need might be her top-of-mind, immediate one if you ask her. But for all of us, the real need is to connect with the Father's love. Sometimes felt needs are doors into people's hearts where the Father can meet them.

As you pray, God begins to touch her. Her eyes fill with tears, and one trickles down her cheek. She becomes very silent, and her composure changes the way it does when you receive important news. Her body stands to attention. The peace of God is settling. At the cash register, a divine transaction is happening. God is dealing with his daughter.

This is ultimately everyone's greatest need, to have an encounter with God. This is what the seventy-two facilitated. The goal of praying for people is an encounter with God. When this becomes your goal, praying for people is suddenly doable. All you do is try to facilitate a moment with God. It's up to him to show up. This takes the pressure off you to say the right words or ensure a miracle or answer every spiritual question they've ever had. And like the seventy-two, great joy will abound.

When God shows up, help the person understand what happened. The seventy-two explained that the kingdom of God was near. Your job is to interpret what's going on. This is how you preach the gospel through prayer.

What if you need some courage? What if praying for strangers sounds like a big, tough thing? What if you feel more cowardly than courageous? Here are five ways to increase your courage so you can pray for people on the spot.

» *Spend time with Jesus.* In Acts 4, Peter and John were arrested for preaching about Jesus. When the rulers saw the courage of these disciples, they were amazed. Why? Because Peter and John were "uneducated" and "untrained" men, former fishermen. But their courage was remarkable. Why were they so brave? Because they had been with Jesus.

» *Bring someone with you.* When Jesus sent the disciples into towns, it was in pairs. It's easier to have courage when someone is with you. When it's just you, it's easy to back down. When it's just you, the risk exists only in your head. No one will know if you retreat. But two can stand in agreement. Your partner can keep you accountable.

» *Take an immediate step in the direction of risk.* It might not be time to move full-speed ahead, but take a step in that direction. When you inch toward the risk, you're closer to accomplishing it. Taking a step creates momentum. The hardest step is the first one. So do something that moves you closer—enlist accountability, say it out loud, schedule it on the calendar. Failure to risk occurs most often because you didn't take the first step.

» *Reject comfort.* Risk is hard because it disrupts comfort. You like the way things are. But risk is unknown and unpredictable. It rocks your nest. But don't worry, you won't have to risk for too long, and soon you'll be back in your recliner with your remote. But for now, reject comfort. Prepare yourself for how comfort will call you back. Be ready for the objections screamed at you.

» *Partner with the Holy Spirit.* The apostle Paul didn't know what he'd say, but the Holy Spirit filled his mouth (Ephesians 6:19). The Holy Spirit will give you words too. You don't have to worry. Your part is opening your mouth. Let the Holy Spirit fill it. This removes pressure from having to say the right thing and puts the pressure back on God. Your role is to show up.

You can increase your courage. With more courage, you'll take more risks in praying for people. By praying for people, you'll facilitate encounters with God that reunite the Father with his children. Why should your wild friend have all the fun?

Tweets from this Chapter

» A secret to asking God for something is to just do it. You don't get if you don't ask. @CSHeinz

» A problem in prayer is asking for what you already have, what you can do on your own, or what you already see. This isn't faith. @CSHeinz

» God won't slap you when you draw near. He'll pull you into his strong, loving arms, which are iron and velvet at once. @CSHeinz

» Learn to ask for what you want God to do, but submit to his will when you do. @CSHeinz

» Sometimes felt needs are doors into people's hearts where the Father can meet them. @CSHeinz

» The goal of praying for people is an encounter with God. When this becomes your goal, then praying for people is suddenly doable. @CSHeinz

» When God shows up, help the person understand what happened. Interpret for them. This is how you preach the gospel through prayer. @CSHeinz

» Failure to risk occurs most often because you didn't take the first step. @CSHeinz

Discussion Questions

1. What is the definition of petition prayer?
2. Have you ever prayed for a stranger in public? How did it go?
3. What are the four secrets to petition prayer?
4. Why can you be bold in prayer?
5. Do you pray more in faith or by sight?
6. Do you think you ask God for too much, too little, or just the right amount?
7. When you pray, do you think of coming as a child to the Father?
8. If your goal were to facilitate an encounter with God, would you pray for people more often?
9. How aware are you of the needs around you?
10. Do you feel drawn to this prayer type?

3
Intercessory Prayer

As the intercessor remains united to him by abiding
in him, his power operates through the intercessor
and accomplishes what needs to be done.
—Norman Grubb, *Rees Howells, Intercessor*[8]

[Anna] never left the temple but worshipped
night and day, fasting and praying.
—Luke 2:37

Definition of Intercessory Prayer: God leading you to pray for the
needs of a person, place, or cause

Bible Character: Anna

W
HAT TIME IS IT? YOU wake up, and it's still dark outside.
You look at the clock, 3:00 a.m. What are you doing
up? Your friend comes to mind, urgently. You need to pray for

him. Pray for him? It's 3:00 a.m.! Can't it wait for later? No, you
don't think so. The urgency is too great. But if you get up now,
you'll be lagging and dragging by afternoon.

You roll over and try to go back to sleep. But you can't. Your
friend keeps returning to your mind. You can't shake the sense
he needs prayer right now. If the roles were switched, he'd pray
for you. Fine, you're awake anyway, so you throw the covers to
the side and climb out of bed. You head downstairs and position
yourself.

But you still don't know what to pray. You haven't spoken
with him for a while. All you know is that he's on a mission trip
in Japan. He's traveling alone. But that's all you know. Big deal,
he's been on mission trips before. He's traveled alone before. He's
not a big baby; he can take care of himself. What in the world are
you supposed to pray? And why now?

So you pray some general prayers for health and safety. Then
suddenly a peculiar picture comes to mind. Are you dreaming?
No, you're kneeling, and you've just pinched yourself to make
sure you're awake. Ouch.

In the picture, you see your friend. He's lying on a bed, but
the thing is, he's flat, really flat. He looks like he's been flattened
by a steamroller. He's paper-thin, barely there. Clearly he needs
help, but what can you do?

Pray for air! Yes, air would be good. If you were flat like that,
you'd want air too. And you wouldn't want to be so thin. So you
pray for God to fill him with air, and as you do, the picture changes.
Suddenly, an air pump appears. An air pump? Now you're certainly
dreaming. So you pinch yourself again. You're not. Ouch, stop
that!

With each word you pray, his body inflates with air, and
soon he's back to normal size. You feel like your job is done. You
e-mail your friend to report what happened. You wonder what

he'll say. Will he block future e-mails from you? Will he call you crazy? But soon you receive an amazing reply.

He explains that the moment his plane landed in Japan, he had trouble breathing. He had had no history of respiratory issues, no report of asthma, but for some reason, he couldn't catch his breath. His health was threatening the entire mission, and he considered canceling his trip.

But for no reason at all, his breathing improved, and he felt stronger and decided to stay. This was the exact time you were praying. This is the prayer of intercession.

In intercessory prayer (or intercession), God leads you to pray for the needs of a person, place, or cause. At first, you don't know what to pray, but God shows you. Can you see how this is different from petition prayer? In petition prayer, you see a need and pray for it, but in intercession, God shows you the need so you can pray for it. In petition prayer, the burden to pray originates from within, but in intercession, the burden originates with God. Intercession is God-led prayer.

Luke 2:36–38 tells about Anna, an eighty-four-year-old widow who was also a prophetess. She only gets three verses in the Bible, but they're packed with information because this little lady packed a punch. After seven years of marriage, Anna's husband died, and she became a widow. According to the Bible, Anna moved into the temple, and "she never left the temple but worshipped night and day, fasting and praying" (Luke 2:37).

That's two prayer types mentioned by name—prophetic prayer and praise. Then verse 38 mentions a third type—it says she gave thanks. Although three types are mentioned explicitly, there's a fourth here that is not mentioned by name. The verse only says she fasted and prayed. So Anna prophesied, she praised, she gave thanks—and she also interceded. Anna was an intercessor.

Intercession is marked by three qualities—intimacy, guidance, and identification—and you see them in Anna's life, in three short verses. Although the words allotted for her are scarce, Luke decided to devote space to Anna's lineage because, to Luke, her lineage was important. Verse 36 says she was the daughter of Phanuel of the tribe of Asher. Phanuel means "face of God." Thus, Anna was the daughter of the face of God.

The first quality—and perhaps the most important—is intimacy. Intimacy is a hallmark of intercession. Intimacy is sharing one's deepest nature; it's marked by close connection. Anna had experienced marriage, the closest relationship between two human beings who are different from each other, man and woman. But then her husband died. As a widow, Anna moved to the temple, God's house, and she experienced closeness with God who was even more different from her. It's like she was then married to God.

Anna spent seven years with her husband, so if she was married at age sixteen, up to this point in the Scripture, she was married to God for sixty-one years. Anna never left the temple but prayed and fasted all the time. She craved the presence of God so much that God's house became her house.

Anna could have written Psalm 84:1–2, 10,

> How lovely is your dwelling place, O LORD Almighty!
>
> My soul yearns, even faints for the courts of the LORD;
>
> My heart and my flesh cry out for the living God…
>
> Better is one day in your courts than a thousand elsewhere;

I would rather be a doorkeeper in the house of
my God

than dwell in the tents of the wicked.

Oh child of the face of God, Oh child who longs for God.
Anna just wanted to be where God was. She made God's holy
place her place. She made God's presence her surroundings.
Although she fasted from earthly food, she feasted on heavenly
food. God was her provision.

You know what it's like to crave the presence of God. You've
been praying before, and suddenly, everything disappeared. All that
remained was God and you—it was simply the two of you. All that
mattered was what he said, what he promised. All that mattered was
what he did, what he was doing. All that mattered was God.

You were at once like the dark, barren world before it was
made, still formless and empty and void. Then slowly and surely
there was activity, wind swooshing over water, the Spirit of God.
Then a voice and then light and the judgment of goodness; not
empty anymore. God filled you, and you could breathe.

There was a season when you moved out of the house you
shared with your friends and moved into an apartment by yourself.
You had come into a sacred closeness with God and needed to
discover him although you had already known him for quite
some time. It seemed to be a period of open heavens, and you
wanted to swim in it and savor it. Oh how sweet it was, the sweet
presence of God.

Your friends didn't hear from you. They left messages on your
answering machine to make sure you weren't dead. But you were
coming alive.

You had long conversations, God and you. You wrote down
what he said, drank his deep words, bathed in his affections. You
asked questions, wondered aloud, examined his responses. You

even danced for him, danced for him in your apartment so that it shook the lights below. That's what the landlord said. And you sang, turned on music and sang to him. That's also what the landlord said.

The intercessor loves God and knows his face. She spends long and deep periods of time with God and has the key to God's house.

After Luke introduces Anna, he says what she did. True to Jewish custom, Joseph and Mary brought baby Jesus to the temple to be purified when he was only eight days old. But Anna, fresh from praying and fasting, walked up to baby Jesus and recognized that he was the Messiah for whom Israel had been longing.

There was no outward indication that this baby was the Savior, the Redeemer of Jerusalem. There were no angels or halos or Messiah business cards. There was just a soft and wrinkled baby. But because she had been with God, Anna was able to recognize God. The presence of God created an awareness of God.

When describing Anna's lineage, Luke not only says she was the daughter of Phanuel, he also says she was from the tribe of Asher. This is good information. The land that was devoted to the tribe of Asher was narrow land, but it was fertile land. The land of Asher was known to be well suited for olive orchards and vineyards. Olive orchards produce olive oil, the substance that represents the Holy Spirit and anointing. Vineyards produce wine, the substance that represents God's covenant and revelation.

The second mark of intercession is guidance by the Holy Spirit. The intercessor watches for the movement and anointing of the Holy Spirit and listens for revelation. Anna had no natural means of knowing the baby was the Messiah, but through her continual intercession for the redemption of Israel, she became wise to the ways of the Spirit so when the Redeemer appeared, she recognized him.

Narrow is the way of the Spirit and few are they who walk in it, but it is fertile. Those who go this uncommon way prosper with oil and new wine. Unlike petition, intercession is based on guidance from the Holy Spirit. Jesus called the Holy Spirit the Counselor, the one to guide you into truth. Jesus said he must leave so the Advocate could come. The Holy Spirit is God's communicator, the agent of divine speech. The Holy Spirit reminds you of the words of Jesus and helps you to comprehend the mind of God. The Holy Spirit is the intercessor's guide and friend.

The Holy Spirit leads you into intercession. If you want to become an intercessor, befriend the Holy Spirit. Welcome the Spirit to land on you like a dove and move in such a way that the dove remains on your shoulder. Create a pleasant place for the Spirit to dwell, and he will build a habitation. Walk in obedience from one step to the next. Incarnation and habitation are different. Jesus incarnated because of sin, but the Holy Spirit inhabits because of obedience.

There are a number of ways the Spirit guides you. He might show you a picture in your mind, also called a vision. In the Bible, Peter, Daniel, and Isaiah all had visions. Through a vision, God can reveal to you what to pray. Think of it as a sign from God. When your minister friend in Japan needed prayer, God sent a sign in the form of a picture.

Buck was in a home church meeting. He felt like God wanted him to pray for someone, but he didn't know for whom. He glanced around the circle, and as soon as his eyes met a man across from him, he saw a picture in his mind. It was a beaver—buckteeth, spatula tail, and all. The beaver was building a home.

So Buck pressed into God, asking him what the beaver meant. He felt impressed to pray that the man would build into his family and home. Buck felt God wanted the man to make more of a commitment to leading his family spiritually. So he prayed for these things.

When the worship service ended, Buck introduced himself to the man and explained what happened. The man said he was an architect, had six children, and had been neglecting his family because of work. God had been convicting him of this already, and Buck's prayers put the fear of God in him. The beaver had been the sign.

Sometimes God sends a word. You might see or hear a word or phrase in your mind in connection to someone like "I am faithful" or "Fear of death" or "Power." So like Buck did with the beaver, you press into God. You pray that God would prove to be faithful or that God would deliver the person from fear of death or pray for more power.

Or God might send a word from the Bible. A biblical reference might ring in your ear or flash in your mind, such as "Deuteronomy 31:6," so you look it up, and it says, "Never will I leave you; never will I forsake you." Or as you're reading your Bible one day, you feel prompted to pray a particular verse for Kate. You see her face in your mind or hear her name whispered in your spirit, so you pray that verse for her. This is how the Spirit leads.

But God doesn't always send a vision or word. Sometimes he sends a burden. It's like labor before birth. So birth it! Suddenly, you have a heavy sense that something needs to be prayed through. It can come as a quickening in your spirit, a feeling of dread, or a cause that holds your attention. You must pray.

You slow down and steady yourself, pleading with God to bring deliverance. He might bring more definition, might fill in the blanks through your pleading. Or he might not. You might never find out why you were called to pray. What's important, however, is praying until the burden lifts. You wouldn't stop laboring for a natural birth until the baby is born, so keep interceding until the spiritual burden lifts—and the baby is born.

When Anna saw the baby Jesus, she immediately knew he was the Messiah. As a Jew, she had prayed for the redemption of Jerusalem. She knew Israel needed salvation. She knew God promised to send a Savior to her nation. And she knew God would send a Savior to her. When Anna prayed in the temple for the Messiah, she prayed with identification as one from Israel.

Identification is another quality of intercession. Through personal initiative or God-sent means, the intercessor identifies with the person, place, or cause of her intercession. The key in identification is to share in their feelings or situation so that it creates understanding in you. And with understanding, you're more likely to pray through the burden until the burden is lifted. There are a variety of ways to create empathy in order to pray for a person, place, or cause—post a picture, do research, read direct correspondence, talk to someone in a similar position, or actually live the way they do.

Rees Howells was an intercessor who lived in Wales in the 1900s. He brought thousands of people in Europe and Africa to Christ and started the Bible College of Wales. But despite his upfront and public activities, Howells's main ministry was intercession.

He had a particular burden for the homeless people in his village. As he began to pray for them, God "called him to share in the physical sufferings of the destitute, which would touch his body. He was to learn a little how to feel as they felt and sit where they sat."[9] The homeless people were served two meager meals a day by the government boarding house, so that's what Mr. Howells ate —soup, bread, and cheese—two times each day. He ate one meal in the morning before going to work in the coalmines and ate the other when he returned home. At first, it was a struggle, but according to Howells, "The Lord has so changed my appetites that I preferred those two meals a day to the four I used to have. That craving for food was taken out of me, and through the whole period, my health was better than anyone else's."[10] That period lasted two and a half years.

Howells found a way to identify with the people he prayed for. He felt their burdens as his own. He was able to pray with understanding. He operated by mercy and compassion. As a result, many people were helped and received eternal life. "The Holy Ghost put such love in our hearts toward these people that we would rather be without ourselves than allow them to be in want," said Howells.

Sometimes you find ways to identify with those you intercede for, but other times God helps you identify with them.

Once in church you felt convinced that God wanted you to pray for physical healing, but you didn't know for whom or about what ailments to pray. Suddenly, your lower back started to ache, and although it hadn't hurt before, now it was tingling. You realized God was directing you to pray for a person with back pain.

So you announced this, and a woman came forward, crying, and asked if you would pray for her, as her lower back had hurt for years. She didn't know what initially had brought the pain on, but it had stolen her life from her. So you began to pray, and God showed you that she was holding onto bitterness and unforgiveness had twisted her heart. That poison had preserved the pain. So you asked her to forgive her offender, and she finally did. Her back became untwisted—the pain was gone.

Another time, a man asked you to pray for him, and as you did, your lips began to taste sweet like the residue of a lollipop. You hadn't had anything sweet to eat or drink. You asked God what that was, and he said he wanted to give him the gift of tongues. When you started praying, it wasn't your intention to pray for that, but God was directing you, so you did.

Because the intercessor is intimate with God and is led by the Holy Spirit, she willingly identifies with the person, place, or cause of intercession so God can have his way.

Anna the intercessor spent day and night in God's presence, which prepared her to intercede for her people. But when she saw the baby Jesus, she realized he was the hope of Israel. The Great Intercessor had come.

Throughout Jesus' life, he stayed connected with the Father. At twelve years of age, Jesus returned to the temple with his parents, but when they left, he stayed behind to "be in his Father's house" (Luke 2:49). As an adult, Jesus often went away to spend time with God. He said the Father and he were one. Jesus pursued intimacy with God.

Jesus was also led by God. He followed the Spirit into the desert. He said the Lord was upon him and only did what the Father was doing. In the garden of Gethsemane, Jesus asked God if the cup could be passed from him, but only if God willed it. So when the cup led to the cross—the Father's will—Jesus drank from it.

And Jesus identified with the objects of his intercession. The Son of God became a man, the ultimate identification. He took the form of a slave and humbled himself to the point of death on the cross. Jesus was tempted in every way so he could identify with humanity. And not only identify, but redeem. He was, as Anna recognized, the redemption of the world.

You can't get to God on your own, not by a million hours on a treadmill, not by feeding all the hungry children, not by lifelong learning. You can't do it by racial reconciliation or by centering yourself or by involuntary poverty. The right clothes won't do it, nor the right house or the right spouse. Neither will being nice to your neighbor or finally loving yourself or going to church on Christmas and Easter (or twice a week).

If you break one of God's commands, you break them all. And when you break them all (or just one), here's what will happen.

You'll stand before God on judgment day, and he'll have no choice but to condemn you. You don't fault an earthly judge for upholding the law, so you can't fault the heavenly judge for doing the same. However, out of God's beautiful, bottomless mercy, he sent Jesus to be your intercessor.

No one but Jesus could stand in the gap because no one but Jesus lived a sinless life. He, unlike you, had a perfect record. He had, unlike you, never lied or stolen or lusted. He had never gossiped or slandered or done the wrong thing. But you're guilty of breaking the entire law, no matter how popular or religious or skinny you are.

So here's what will happen. When you pass from this earth, you'll appear before God. He'll show you every offense you ever committed, every stinking last one. He'll shake his head very sadly and say, "I'm sorry. Your sins have condemned you." A tear will drop from his eye. It will become very silent and still.

But then Jesus will step forward. The rustling of his feet will break the silence, and he'll say, "Yes, that's true. But my blood covers her. She has been redeemed."

And heaven will break out in chorus.

And you'll run to your Father, who was once your judge, and he'll say, "You're home now," and you'll enjoy eternity with him because on the earth you recognized and received the Redeemer.

Tweets from this Chapter

» In petition prayer, you see a need and pray for it, but in intercession, God shows you the need so you can pray for it. @CSHeinz

» Intercession is marked by three qualities: intimacy, guidance, and identification. @CSHeinz

» The intercessor loves God and knows his face. She spends long and deep periods of time with him and has the key to his house. @CSHeinz

» Incarnation and habitation are different. Jesus incarnated because of sin, but the Holy Spirit habitates because of obedience. @CSHeinz

» In intercession, God doesn't always send a vision or word. Sometimes he sends a burden that is like labor unto birth. So birth it! @CSHeinz

» You can't get to God on your own, not by hours on the treadmill or feeding hungry children or lifelong learning. By Christ alone. @CSHeinz

» Sometimes you find ways to identify for whom you intercede, but other times God helps you identify with them. @CSHeinz

Discussion Questions

1. What is the definition of intercession?
2. How is intercession different from petition prayer?
3. What are the three qualities of intercession?
4. What is evidence of intimacy with God in Anna's life?
5. What did Anna recognize about the baby Jesus?
6. Can you recall a time when you were led into intercession? How did God lead you?
7. How does identification benefit you in intercession?
8. What qualified Jesus to intercede for humanity?
9. How can you create an atmosphere for intercession?
10. Do you feel drawn to this prayer type?

4

Prophetic Prayer

A prophetic word seems so often to come at just the
right time in a person's life, at that moment when
there is a need to know God is near, that he cares,
that he still loves and guides and answers prayer.
—Sam Storms, *The Beginner's Guide to Spiritual Gifts*[11]

You must go to everyone I send you to
and say whatever I command you.
—Jeremiah 1:7

Definition of Prophetic Prayer: Receiving a message from God
for someone else

Bible Character: Jeremiah

O NE EVENING, YOU'RE CLEANING UP after dinner. As you
wash the silverware, you sense God impressing something

on your heart. You know what his voice sounds like, your shepherd making himself known. It's the fruit of your relationship over the years—you know when he's calling. Regardless of your life's season—obedience when you remained near or disobedience when you walked the other way, God's voice has been a constant.

But you haven't always wanted to hear.

He might have called you to change or look at yourself differently. Or take a risk you didn't feel capable of taking or rewrite a long-held belief. With God, there's no telling. There's no controlling the God who likes to communicate. With one swift word, he turned on the lights, and with another, he pushed up the land. With a word, he sent a devastating flood, and with another, he sent his son to die. God's not capricious, but he's not ineffective either.

Perhaps this is why a talking God is not altogether comfortable. When his work is you, you can't sit idle. God's word will work on you, even against your steel will and crossed arms. The soul made by God and for God is being affected. You just don't know it yet.

An alarming thing about God is his full access. Not only does he have the nerve to interfere with your life, he can do it anytime. He doesn't restrict the conversation to church. He talks outside the four walls. He doesn't wait for you to start talking about holy things and then make an entrance. God meets you in the mundane, not only on Sunday but on Monday as well. And often God comes when you're not expecting him.

It used to drive you nuts, God showing up uninvited. He'd disrupt your routine, change your plans for the evening. But you've learned to roll with it. Talking with his creation is certainly within God's rights. This is what you get with a living God. Your unbelieving friends don't have to deal with such disruptions. Their dead and mute gods, or no gods at all, don't try to change them. They're not about to challenge them. It's easier for your friends this way. They're free to live like they want. They're free from divine inconvenience.

But not you. You bought into God's offer, which came with God himself—God unfiltered, unrestricted, unregulated. You gave God full permission to interfere and interrupt and disrupt. So even though the dishes are high and the grease is hardening and you were planning on taking a long bubble bath, God comes to you at the sink. You stop everything and listen.

He says you ought to buy flowers for someone.

"Flowers?" you ask.

"Yes, flowers," he answers.

He doesn't tell you for whom, but he tells you it has to be tonight. You should leave the dishes and go now. So much for your bath. The disruptive God has spoken.

You drive to the flower store. You still don't know who the intended recipient is, but you think God wants you to buy three roses and a card. As you pay for them, your particular neighbor comes to mind. Peculiar, you haven't seen her in a while, but yes, you feel very strongly the flowers are for her.

You sit inside your car to write on the card. You ask God what to write, and then you write what you think God wants to say to her. "I'm well pleased with you" is how you fill the white, empty space. Then you drive to your neighbor's house and knock on the door. There are butterflies in your stomach. Why should you feel nervous giving a gift to her?

The neighbor opens the door, and you hand her the roses and card. The neighbor is surprised. She takes the gift, thanks you shortly, and quickly shuts the door. *That's it?* you think. You want to know what's going on, why the flowers and the card, why the urgent delivery. But there are no answers tonight. Just dirty dishes and solid grease in the sink.

In prophetic prayer, you receive a message from God for someone else. Prophetic prayer has four components:

» God

» Message

» Messenger

» Recipient

First, there's God, who initiates the process. Unless he speaks, prophetic prayer doesn't happen. He's the mover, the cause behind this type of prayer. Through prophetic prayer, God demonstrates that he's a communicator. The same God who spoke the world into existence continues to speak. Why? Because there's more he wants to say.

Second, there's the message. This is the content that is spoken by God. The message always conforms to his written word or his character. The purpose of the message is to encourage, strengthen, and solidify.

Third, there's the messenger. God speaks the message to someone he can trust. He has other means of communicating. God could get on a loudspeaker, draw in sand, or speak through your dachshund. But sometimes God uses messengers to deliver his word. They don't always get it right—using human messengers introduces the possibility of error—but nonetheless, God has decided to use prophetic prayer.

And finally, there's the recipient. The recipient is the person for whom the message is intended.

One of the most well-known messengers in the Bible is Jeremiah. God told him that before he was born, God made him a messenger. But Jeremiah questioned. "I don't know how to speak; I am only a child" (Jeremiah 1:6). The messenger doubted God's plan. But God didn't.

He told him, "You must go to everyone I send you to and say whatever I command you. Do not be afraid of them, for I am with you" (Jeremiah 1:7–8).

To answer Jeremiah's doubt, God said three things:

> » I'll be with you.

> » I'll tell you what to say.

> » Don't be afraid.

This is essentially what God does every time he sends you on a mission. He promises his presence. He'll be with you all the way. God's presence provides you with all you need.

And God tells you what to say. The mission is God's idea in the first place. He has orchestrated the movement, positioned the players, and timed it just right. It's really God's mission after all, and he's inviting you to participate. So the pressure is off. You don't have to manufacture the razzle-dazzle, pull out the magic, and hope it works. You just have to trust and obey.

So there's no need to fear. God says don't be afraid but rather have courage. Courage is action powered by trusting God. When you're moved by fear, you don't trust God. You trust in the things that make you afraid. But when God is with you, there's no need to fear.

So what was Jeremiah so worried about?

> » He looked at his youth.

> » He looked at his weakness.

> » He looked at the people to whom he would be sent.

And this caused him to doubt and back off from his calling.

But God reassured him, "I will be with you" (Jeremiah 1:8). So Jeremiah went and said what God wanted him to say. And God was with him.

But you're no Jeremiah. Why does God do it this way?

One of the reasons God uses messengers is to get your attention. Sometimes you're not listening when God is trying to speak. You're stuck in your routine, running from one thing to another, and you don't recognize when God is speaking to you directly. Or you don't think you're worth God's attention. You're prone to shame or guilt or perfectionism. And because you don't measure up, you think God has nothing for you. But God has much to say, and when he can't get through, he might reach out to you through messengers.

He disrupts your walls and little shelters you have erected to preserve yourself. You may not be living the abundant life, but it's the life you know, so don't mess with it. Remove a leg, and the structure will collapse. So stay out. But God's a meddler. He meddles in your life and your neighbor's and others he wants to bring close. His word crashes through and breaks down those self-erected barriers.

And when they do, it reminds you that God is a living God. He's alive today just as much as he ever was, and not only alive, involved.

For example, for years your grandpa thought that God made the world and then stepped away. He thought God was a father who watched his kids play in the pool but never got wet with them. Until one day God proved that he had been close all along.

He visited Grandpa one night. Until then, Grandpa was unable to lift his arms above his shoulders and kick his legs back and forth. But God showed up, and suddenly, Grandpa could. Then God spoke a message to Grandpa, secret and tender and meaningful. In an instant, it undid the notions of divine distance and civility. Why would a civil God come so close? Get messy with creation? Get wet?

Finally, Grandpa understood that God was close.

The Christ followers in the family had been saying this for years. But he didn't believe them. Until now. And now Grandpa wants his story told.

"But what if people say these are the ramblings of an old man?" you ask.

"They might, but they can't deny what happened to my body."

Then he said, "Besides, the healing might go away, but I'm so grateful to have had this experience."

And when Grandpa died six months later, he went to God's arms, which weren't far away.

Another reason for prophecy is that God's nature is to communicate. The persons of the Godhead are highly social. God began creating the world by speaking four words, "Let there be light" (Genesis 1:3). Jesus is called the Word of God in John 1:1. The Greek word is *logos,* which means "divine speech or message."[12] The job of the Holy Spirit is to reveal the words of Jesus (John 16:13). One of the ways that humans are made in God's image (Genesis 1:27) is by reflecting God's social nature. And even nature itself mirrors God. Psalm 19 says the skies declare God's glory and pour forth speech. So when you communicate, you reflect the essence of the God who made you.

Through prophecy, God speaks because he cares about you. When God speaks, you know you're on his mind. One word from God can reassemble the world as you know it. You end up feeling closer to God because he has spoken. Wow, with so much to do, he still cares for you! And think of all the people whining and moaning and carrying on. But God has set his heart on you nonetheless. God is not sitting at the edge of the pool with his phone and book, glancing up now and then. He's body-deep in the water, launching you from his arms, and having tea parties with you underneath.

God uses prophecy when he has more to say than is in the Bible. When the Bible was canonized in 1546, God didn't stop talking. Yes, the Bible is the hands-down, authoritative word of God. There is nothing to be added to it and nothing to be taken away. But remember, God's nature is to communicate.

For example, the Bible didn't tell you to pray for your flattened friend who lost his breath in Japan. The Bible didn't say the architect ought to build into his family. The Holy Spirit did—in addition to the Bible. God will not contradict his written word. His spoken word will always resonate and agree with his written word, but he doesn't limit his speech to the Bible.

God uses prophecy to benefit the common good, which is the church and the world. Prophecy can open the heart of an unbeliever. First Corinthians 14:1 says, "Follow the way of love and eagerly desire spiritual gifts, especially the gift of prophecy." Eagerly desire prophecy, why? Because God gives spiritual gifts, including prophecy, in order to benefit the common good (1 Corinthians 12:7). This explains why God says to follow the way of love and why the functions of prophecy are to strengthen, encourage, and comfort (1 Corinthians 14:3).

So what is the common good? That the believing church and the unbelieving world would know God. Prophecy is meant to be practiced not only in church but also in the world. Believers aren't supposed to be the only beneficiaries of God's voice; unbelievers are to benefit as well. First Corinthians 14:24–25 says, "But if an unbeliever or someone who does not understand comes in while everybody is prophesying, he will be convinced by all that he is a sinner and will be judged by all, and the secrets of his heart will be laid bare."

Do you get what's happening here? An unbeliever experienced prophecy. The believers didn't hush-hush their prophetic words. They didn't stop because an unbeliever was there and might think it was weird or off-putting. They let the power of God work. Isn't that what unbelievers want to know? If God is for real? If God can offer something the world cannot?

In response, "[The unbeliever] will fall down and worship God exclaiming, 'God is really among you!'" (1 Corinthians 14:25). This is what prophecy can do for an unbeliever! It can show that God knows them.

Another reason God uses prophecy is to bring the church into healthy community. One of the ways the Bible explains the church is to say it is a body with many parts (Romans 12:4–5). Every part functions differently. "If a man's gift is prophesying, let him use it in proportion to his faith. If it is serving, let him serve; if is it teaching, let him teach" (Romans 12:6). Only when each part functions properly can the body function as a whole. So when God creates messengers and attaches them to the body, it's for everyone's benefit.

Yes, messengers hear from God, but they don't have God in their pockets. Messengers need the other members too. No one person has everything that God has to offer or the complete counsel of God. The body removes the lone cowboy mentality. No messenger stands on his or her own. Sometimes messengers get it wrong when they communicate what they think they heard from God. There will be mistakes.

But that's the reason for checks and balances. The prophetic message ought to confirm God's word and character because prophecy is the testimony of Jesus (Revelation 19:10). The prophetic message ought to be brought before community by the recipient to help confirm and interpret it. The prophetic message might not be for action right now. And the prophetic message is sometimes conditional upon obedience. For these reasons, the messenger checks his motives when delivering the prophetic word.

» Are you delivering the message so people will think you're highly spiritual?

» Are you speaking what God has said to climb the church ladder?

» Are you sharing a word to correct someone you don't like?

» Are you correcting someone to cover your own sin?

There are three ways prophecy functions. *The first is as a spiritual gift (Romans 12:6).* This means that God has given the gift of prophecy to an individual for regular and effective use for the common good. In general, spiritual gifts can be exercised at the will of the individual. However, prophecy depends on God speaking the message first.

The second way prophecy functions is as an anointing (Numbers 11:25). An anointing is a special enabling given by God for a period of time. In a prophetic anointing, people who don't have the gift of prophecy still receive messages from God for others. This anointing might fall on an individual during a prayer time. Or it might fall on a group of people all at once for a period of time. The Bible says to be eager to prophesy, so although not all people receive the gift of prophecy, they can still prophesy through the anointing. When and how the anointing arrives depends on God.

The third way is as an office (Ephesians 4:11). An office is an official position that carries special responsibilities. The particular person might vacate the office, but the office still remains. In the church, God has appointed certain individuals to be prophets. Their position carries responsibilities that are beyond the spiritual gift of prophecy. Every office of prophet begins with the gift of prophecy, but not everyone gifted in prophecy is recognized as a prophet. The biblical prophets hold a special position because their prophecies are canonized in the Bible.

One morning, you're reading the Bible and praying. You're not praying about anything in particular, sort of volleying prayers to God as they come up. Suddenly, your skinny friend comes to mind, and you feel an urge to pray for her. You haven't spoken with her lately, but you know she has recently started a ministry to strippers at the local strip club.

Such a delicate ministry, you think, so you pray for wisdom and direction. Then you sense that God is getting ready to speak, so you get ready. You ask God what he has to say.

You begin to hear a message, not audibly, but you hear it inside you, in the place where God usually meets you. That place has been pruned and cultivated through years of relationship, and you know the sound of his voice. You call it your holy place.

As you hear the message, you write it down. You've learned to have a pen and paper ready for occasions like this. A good messenger is always prepared. You finish the message, and ask if God's done. You think so.

You read through it. It sounds biblical. It sounds like something God would say. No red flags here. You move to the next step.

You ask him if this message is meant for praying or for sharing. This is important to ask. Sometimes God has spoken to you for the purpose of praying, not for sharing. Sometimes, he wanted you to pray for a season and then share it. And other times he wanted you to share it right away. You think you ought to share this one now.

So you have another decision to make—how to share it with your skinny friend. There are lots of possibilities. You could call or send a letter, e-mail, or text. You could request a meeting with her. The delivery method should be appropriate for the relationship and tone of the message.

But you keep the message to yourself. It's not meant to share with the world. You don't post on Facebook, "Listen to what God just told me for my skinny friend!" It's a private matter between her and God, and because God brought you into it, he trusts you to treat it right.

You decide to e-mail her. You type out the message, which is easy because you have written it down. You encourage her to pray through it and to share it with the community that can help confirm and interpret it. Then you let it go.

It's vital to let the package go once it reaches its destination. The package was never yours to begin with. You're a messenger. It's not your responsibility to see the message fulfilled. It's not your job to make sure she's doing whatever the message said. You're neither the prophecy police nor skinny girl's mom.

You hit "Send." You might never hear back about this, and that's okay. You feel satisfied for doing your job. But you do hear back. She says she's crying and crying. The message resonates so strongly with God's pull on her heart. She wants her ministry to be God's ideas, not a bunch of good ideas. She wants God's heart to lead the team.

Oh, and she's about to board a plane for Las Vegas to attend a conference for ministries like hers. She says there will be plenty of good ideas. But that's not what she's after because God has shown his heart.

What a privilege for you to deliver God's messages!

You finally see your neighbor, so maybe now you'll hear her story. She clutches your hands while tears drop from her eyes, and as she talks, you begin to cry too. Just recently, her husband walked out on her after twenty years of marriage without explanation or warning, nothing. He just walked out. For the first time in years, she is alone.

But God had not forgotten her. He saw her loneliness. And

seeing her loneliness, God spoke to you about buying her flowers. And he said it had to be that night because, although her husband would not be giving her flowers, God would. It was her twentieth wedding anniversary.

Tweets from this Chapter

» God's Word will work on you, even against your steel will and crossed arms. The soul made by God and for God is being affected. @CSHeinz

» An alarming thing about God is his full access. Not only does he have the nerve to interfere with your life, he can do it anytime. @CSHeinz

» God could get on a loud speaker, draw in sand, speak through your dachshund. But sometimes God uses messengers to deliver his word. @CSHeinz

» When God speaks, you're reminded that he cares for you. This word can reassemble the world as you know it. @CSHeinz

» God uses prophecy when he has more to say than is in the Bible. When the Bible was canonized in 1546, God didn't stop talking. @CSHeinz

» God uses prophecy to benefit the common good, which is the church and the world. Prophecy can open the heart of an unbeliever. @CSHeinz

» Prophecy can function in three ways: as a spiritual gift, as an anointing, and as an office. @CSHeinz

Discussion Questions

1. What is the definition of prophetic prayer?
2. What are the four components of prophetic prayer?

3. What did God tell Jeremiah in order to reassure him?

4. Do you think God speaks to you? If so, in what ways?

5. Has God ever showed up invited and ruined your routine?

6. Has God ever given you a message for someone else?

7. Has anyone ever given you a message from God?

8. What are some reasons God uses prophecy?

9. Why is accountability important for messengers and recipients?

10. Do you feel drawn to this type of prayer?

5
Listening Prayer

But whether in the "desert" or at home, hold in
your heart a deep, inner, listening silence and there
be still until the work of solitude is done.
—Richard Foster, *Celebration of Discipline*[13]

Be still and know that I am God.
—Psalm 46:10

Definition of Listening Prayer: Sitting at the feet of Jesus and listening for him

Bible Character: Mary of Bethany

ONE DAY, YOU START THINKING about your smartphone and how attached you are to it. You take it everywhere you go; it's become your grownup umbilical cord. It connects you to life. Your kids see you more with your phone than without it. You wonder what they'll say about you when they're older.

"Dad really knew how to use his phone."

"Dad made the most of his monthly data plan."

If that's the impression you leave on them, you will have failed as a parent. There are other impressions to make: the adventures you had together, the imaginary beasts you slayed, the real places you visited, the songs you sang, the stories you told. But most of all, you want them to say you were present with them, and you listened.

But right now that's not true. Too often your mind is on other things. You said you were listening to their story when you weren't. You said you were watching their skit, but not really. The blue buzz of the phone flashed under the table, your fingers tapped away on the keyboard. You excused yourself to the bathroom. You snuck a peak.

And now you can hear them say, "Dad loved his phone, but what about us?"

So you decide to do something drastic—you'll cut the cord and kiss your beloved phone good-bye.

The next day you head to the phone store.

"Hi, I want to downgrade my smartphone," you tell the clerk. "I don't want e-mail or Internet anymore."

"You want to downgrade?" she answers. "No problem, sir. What a good idea!" But that's just because she's had customer service training. She's been trained to make the customer feel brilliant. But what's she's really thinking is, *L-O-S-E-R! No one downgrades. Everyone upgrades.*

She walks you to a wall of kiddie phones. There are no flashing lights, no neon signs. There are no ads reassuring you that you're making the right choice, you smart and sexy thing. You choose a phone that does what you want it to do—take pictures, play music, and send text messages. Oh, and make phone calls. Making phone calls would be useful in a telephone.

You turn it over in your hands. It looks stupid and already you hate it. What are you supposed to do with this? Make phone calls? You don't want to make phone calls. You want to check e-mail. You want to surf the web. You want to post on Facebook. Dumb phone.

"I guess I'll take this one," you concede, as they all look the same. You pay for your new phone, although they should pay you for taking it off their hands, and you leave the store with the sinking feeling that you've just been conned, hilariously.

At the stoplight, you reach for your phone, but then remember you can't do anything with it. Not anything you would want to do anyway. Maybe you've made a mistake. Maybe you can undo the transaction and reattach your cord. Whatever were you thinking?

Luke 10:38–42 tells the story of Mary and Martha of Bethany. Jesus was a guest in their home, probably along with the other disciples. As guests, they were persons of honor. Hospitality was very important, a cultural responsibility. So Martha set herself to preparing the home for Jesus and the other guests. But not Mary. No, Mary sat at Jesus' feet and listened.

Martha acted like a host, but Mary acted like a guest.

When Martha noticed that Mary wasn't helping her, she said to Jesus, "Don't you care that my sister is doing nothing and I'm doing everything alone? Tell her to help me!"

But Jesus didn't tell Mary to help Martha. Instead he said, "Martha, Martha,"—he said her name not once but twice—"you are worried about many things, but only one thing is needed."

Jesus didn't care about the hospitality or cultural rules or even what Martha would feel or think. He just wanted her to spend time with him. He said, "Mary has chosen what is better, and it will not be taken away from her."

In other words, it's better to sit and listen than to stand and do. Mary and Martha teach that when Jesus is present, it's better to be a guest than a host.

Listening prayer is sitting at the feet of Jesus and listening for him. He might speak; he might not. He might act; he might not. That's not the point. The goal of listening prayer is being silent so that God becomes your only noise. It's to be still and know that he is God (Psalm 46:10). Listening prayer is quieting yourself to the hush of the Almighty so that your soul is satisfied chiefly in Him. You feast in his presence.

Your soul is hungry and pines for nourishment. It roams the space of the earth looking for its fill. And when it finds something it thinks will satisfy, it devours it whole. Then feeling still empty again, not whole, it roams farther out, farther in, farther up, and farther down, ranging the depths and heights for the prize. Busy but not finding.

But Jesus said to eat of him, the manna from heaven, the bread of life.

"Eat my body and drink my blood" (John 6:54), "and you will not be hungry and thirsty again" (John 4:14).

An anointing is a special purpose or enabling to do something particular. The prayer of intercession comes with a *seeking* anointing; the purpose is to seek and be led by God. Prophetic prayer comes with a *sending and saying* anointing; the purpose is to go to whom God sends you and say what he has said to say. But listening prayer comes with a *sitting* anointing. The purpose is to sit and listen for Jesus.

Sounds simple. The easy life, like retiring right after graduating from college. Jumping into your bathrobe from your graduation gown. "If God wants you to lie on a couch and be with him, that's the best place you can be," the wise man said. Yes, sounds easy, but it's not, which means Mary has much to teach you.

She teaches you that while there are cultural norms to obey and acts of service to perform, better still is listening for Jesus. The Bible says that Martha was "distracted by the preparations." Distracted from what? Distracted from what was more important than her preparations.

You might say that sitting in the heat of activity is the distraction. But it's not. The real distraction is doing that which keeps you from sitting with Jesus. Jesus said what Mary did would not be taken away from her. But he didn't say the same to Martha. When anything trumps your devotion to Jesus, it's fair game to be removed. Nothing is more sacred.

Not even service to Jesus is sacred. Jesus would rather you sit with him than serve him. He is more jealous for your presence than he is for your service. Can the same be said about you? Are you more jealous for God's presence than his service?

The one who listens for God has trained her heart to be satisfied in him. It is then that she can be trusted with ministry because the ministry has not become her life. Instead, it will be performed in gratitude and humble desperation because Jesus has become her life. It's the right way around: Jesus first and then everything else. Not everything else and then Jesus.

In Luke 14:26, just a few chapters after the story of Mary and Martha, Jesus threw down one of his most challenging statements ever. He said, "If anyone comes to me and does not hate his father and mother, his wife and children, his brothers and sisters—even his own life—he cannot be my disciple."

Jesus didn't mean you ought to harm your family. That would go against his other teachings. What he meant is that the love you have for God should outweigh, out measure, outshine, and outlast your devotion to others. The measure of your love for God should make your devotion to others seem like hate. It's a matter of comparison.

Your love for God is a redwood; your love for others is a daisy. Your love for God is an ocean; your love for others is a raindrop. Your love for God is the sun; your love for others is a spark. When people look at your life, there should be no doubt as to who your Number One is. It should make them jealous that God gets so much of your attention, creativity, passion, and labor. It should be clear that you're eating of Jesus.

"All of humanity's problems stem from man's inability to sit quietly in a room alone,"[14] said Blaise Pascal.

From not being able to sit quietly in a room with God, you are distracted by other things. You don't always get the order right. You don't listen for Jesus. You love plenty of other things before God. There's a name for them. Idols.

John Calvin said human hearts are perpetual idol factories. They turn out idols in mass quantities, sometimes making new ones, sometimes updating old ones. It's the business you know.

That's because you were made to love God. But you make idols instead. You settle for easy substitutes—heroes on the field and the stage, knowledge and ingenuity, entertainment and consumer goods. Even the sacred cows of Christianity can become idols—serving the poor, caring for orphans, pursuing your calling, finding your story, living in community, enforcing justice, rescuing the needy, or stewarding the earth. And when one idol passes, another takes its place. You're good at your idol-making business.

But God is supposed to be the object of your deepest love, the talk of the town, the talk of your heart. Listening prayer enables you to listen to your heart. It's easier to stand and do rather than sit and listen. You have to pay attention to your emotions. You have no defense to stand behind. Your usual accolades don't do. You have no control, and you have to trust. You're at the mercy of God. He might challenge you to change. When you're distracted from his voice, you remain the same. But not when you're listening.

He might ask you to give something up, go somewhere, do something. He could ask you to surrender a treasure or a trinket, a dream or a desire. He might want you to follow him into the light or into the dark or, worse, into the gray. But your appetite is for entertainment, and this is not that. You get bored with fewer lights and sounds and punch lines.

"My sheep listen to my voice; I know them, and they follow me," Jesus said (John 11:27).

And he also said, "Man does not live by bread alone, but on every word that comes from the mouth of God" (Matthew 4:4).

Listening prayer is perhaps one of the most challenging prayer types because it requires you to strip attachments, let go of performances and just be with God. He might speak. He might not. He might act. He might not. It's just you and God. You're naked before your maker. It's not entirely comfortable.

You have a gimpy little toe that embarrasses you. Over the years it has been battered by athlete's foot and injuries and lately it has turned yellow, thick, and crusty—"a rhino toe," Anne Lamott would call it.

You hide it from daylight; it's your hunchback from Notre Dame, your phantom of the opera. Things are going well, your secret is safe, until one day you nick your foot on the motor blade of your dad's boat. A sharp pain surges through your foot, but worse, through your little toe. Now the toe is screaming for attention. It apparently doesn't like life in the shadows.

You yelp. When the people ask what's wrong, you say nothing, but they know better. The gig is up. You explain what happened, and they instruct you to climb on board so the nurse can look at it—your mom's a nurse. You resist. You say "It's just fine." But they won't relent, so you climb the ladder and stretch out your leg. The phantom removes his mask, so to speak.

Your mom leans in and then steps back and rather medically and diagnostically says, "Hmm, I think something's wrong with your toe." No, really, Clara Barton? That doesn't look normal to you? Florence Nightingale, you don't think toes should look like this? You shrug your shoulders as if you're as surprised as she is. But the truth is, you've known for a long time but haven't done anything to fix it.

The good nurse announces, "I think it's a fungus." Everyone gasps and then takes turns visiting the freak show. Your secret is out: You're damaged and deformed.

Sometimes you resist God because of your deformities. You're ashamed of your gnarled little parts. You've taken some things into hiding, the less flattering pieces—a doubt here, an addiction there, a mistake, a fear, a loathing. How can you sit with God who is perfect, who is holy, who is light? You know you can't hide from God, so instead you delay, you distract, you ignore.

You resist listening as long as you can. But finally, the inevitable can't be put off anymore. You come before your maker, and what does he say?

"This is my child, whom I love."

Listening prayer restores your true self. Normally, you're running around and proving yourself, but now none of that. You realize you are nothing more than a child, and there is no higher place to climb. You're in your daddy's arms. What better place to be? Sitting at his feet reminds you of who you are.

The lesser waits for the greater to speak.

There's an interesting name for God in Genesis 31:42. Jacob says, "The God of my father." Who was Jacob's father? It was Isaac. So this is like saying, "The God of Isaac."

Then he said, "The God of Abraham." Who was Abraham?

Jacob's grandfather, the father of Isaac. But then he said something peculiar.

He called God, "The Fear of Isaac." Then he repeated it a little while later, "So Jacob took an oath in the name of the Fear of his father Isaac" (v. 53). God was the Fear of Jacob's father, Isaac. But why this name for God? To answer this question, go to the story of Abraham and Isaac (Genesis 22:1–19).

God asked Abraham to sacrifice his son Isaac to him. Although Abraham loved his son, he decided to obey God. Abraham packed up wood for the altar and his knife for killing, and he brought his son to the mountain.

Isaac asked his dad what they would sacrifice. Abraham said God would provide the sacrifice. At the top of the mountain, Abraham bound his son and piled him on top of the wood. Just as he was about to slay Isaac, an angel appeared and said, "Stop!" and showed Abraham a ram in the bushes. The angel then said that because Abraham did not withhold even his son from God, God would bless him. Abraham loved God more than his son.

Now imagine Isaac in this experience. What has he learned about God? He has learned that with one word, God could have slayed him. God was fully capable of killing him. God's single command overpowered a father's love for his son. But that's not what God did. With one word, God spared him.

That's why God is the Fear of Isaac. To fear God is to respect and honor him. Yes, he's your daddy, but he's also your Lord. Listening prayer cultivates the fear of the Lord because you wait for the greater one to speak, and when you do, you gain wisdom. "The fear of the LORD is the beginning of wisdom," says Psalm 111:10. If you want to become wise, start listening for Jesus.

It can be unnerving sitting in a room alone. At first you reach for something to thrill you. But when you listen for Jesus, you learn to wait on God, which births patience. You don't learn patience by taking a pill; you learn patience by being in situations that require patience. And once patience has its way in you, you'll be able to wait on God. And when you wait on God, you'll birth patience.

Listening prayer positions you to receive from God himself. If humanity's problems stem from man's inability to sit quietly in a room alone, perhaps man's joys derive from doing just that. When you learn to sit with Jesus and be content in that place, you learn to trust him. And once you trust him, you'll follow him anywhere.

So back to your smartphone story. After almost turning around and returning to the phone store, you decide not to. Now it's been three months since you cut the cord. Surprisingly, the ground hasn't crumbled, and the sky hasn't fallen. Actually, life's been pretty good.

You still dislike your new phone and get jealous at what other people can do with theirs. You even hide it sometimes because you're embarrassed by it. But you're becoming the parent you want to be. You're attentive; you listen.

One morning, your daughter hands you a card she has made. It says, "Dad, thank you for getting a new phone." Your daughter has noticed the change it has made. Her heart is happy.

Now maybe in the future your kids won't mention your affinity for your phone. They'll mention your affinity for them. And maybe God will to.

Tweets from this Chapter

> » Mary and Martha teach us that when Jesus is present, it's better to be a guest than a host. @CSHeinz

> » Listening prayer is being silent so that God becomes your only noise. It's to be still and know that he is God (Psalm 46:10). @CSHeinz

» Listening prayer is quieting yourself to the hush of the Almighty so your soul is satisfied in him. You feast in his presence. @CSHeinz

» When anything trumps your devotion to Jesus, it's fair game to be removed. Nothing is more sacred. @CSHeinz

» The one who listens for God has trained her heart to be satisfied in him. It is then that she can be trusted with ministry. @CSHeinz

» Jesus would rather you sit with him than serve him. He is more jealous for your presence than he is for your service. @CSHeinz

» The measure of your love for God should make your other devotions seem like hate. @CSHeinz

» Listening prayer is hard because it requires you to strip off attachments, let go of performances and just be with God. @CSHeinz

Discussion Questions

1. What is the definition of listening prayer?
2. Who is a person in your life who really listens to you? How do you feel when he or she listens?
3. Who do you relate more to—Mary or Martha? Is it easier for you to be a guest or a host?
4. Is silence challenging for you? Why?
5. Are you more jealous for God's presence or his service?
6. What are some benefits of listening prayer?
7. Have you ever been scared to come before God? Why?

Chris Heinz

8. Are you putting anything ahead of God in your life? What does surrendering it look like?

9. What is distracting you from sitting with Jesus?

10. Do you feel drawn to this prayer type?

6

Fellowship Prayer

It was a great delusion to think that the times of
prayer ought to differ from other times; we are strictly
obliged to adhere to God by action in the time of
action as by prayer in the season of prayer.
—Brother Lawrence, *The Practice of the Presence of God*[15]

Then the man and his wife heard the sound of the LORD God
as he was walking in the garden in the cool of the day.
—Genesis 3:8

Definition of Fellowship Prayer: Spending time with God in an
activity that is not traditionally sacred or prayerful

Bible Characters: Adam and Eve

ALTHOUGH IT TOOK YOU FIVE years to graduate from college,
you're finally done. You move across the country to

California to start a job. There you meet a beautiful woman. She has a smooth way about her, a comfortable disposition that's confident but not cocky, and her name is exotic but not trying too hard. It's correct to say you like her from the start.

She asks if you're a mountain biker and you say yes. This isn't entirely untrue. Truth is, you have a mountain bike. But you're about to learn that having a mountain bike and being a mountain biker are not the same. You make plans to mountain bike together at your next chance. Your next chance rolls around. You call her and decide to meet on Monday.

On Monday, you show up at her apartment, holding your helmet from eighth grade, at least that's how it looks. If you painted a ladybug on it, it wouldn't look strange. Your stark white legs look like they haven't seen the sun in weeks, and your shorts aren't biking shorts. She's starting to think that maybe you're not the mountain biker you said you were.

"Umm, can you help me put my tire back on?" you ask. You had removed the wheel to fit the bike in your car but couldn't figure out how to put it back on. Busted, now she knows you're not a mountain biker. Is this your first time? And from what little girl did you steal that helmet?

But she plays it cool and tosses you a pair of biking shorts. *Her* extra biking shorts. *Spandex* biking shorts. You've never worn spandex biking shorts before, much less those belonging to the girl on your first date. Girl's shorts are cut different from guys.

"Here, put these on. Then put your shorts on top," she instructs.

You head into the bathroom and put on her spandex. In the process, you forget her last instruction. You emerge with her shorts on, your body all squeezed in like a trapped manatee, your shorts *not* on top. You spin around like Miss America posing for the judges.

"How do they look?" you ask.

"Let's just get going," she says flatly. This lady usually bikes from her apartment to the mountain, but because of you, she decides to drive to the mountain instead. After she has put your front tire back on, you throw your bikes into her truck (how cool is that, she has a truck), and you drive to the mountain.

You unload your bikes, and she wants you to go first. You must look so good in spandex that she wants to ride behind you, you tell yourself. You decide to go out fast, show her what you can do. But what is this? Mountain biking has hills? You have to pedal hard? There aren't any chairlifts? You're not used to hills, not used to *hard*. You begin to strain.

She suggests you take a break. "Well, if you really need one," you say. You stop and climb off your bike.

"You don't look so good," she says.

"I don't feel so good," you say.

Then whatever is in your stomach decides it wants out all at once like schoolchildren lining up at the door for summer. You take a step, lean over, and let the kids out. Summer is in session! When you're done, you flop on the ground into a pile of sticky tree sap.

"Sorry about your shorts," you say.

At this point, you're thinking it's reasonable to go home. No one would shame you for packing it in, going home, and sending her shorts back in the mail. But there's something about her, about being together, that you both want to keep going. You climb onto your bikes and start pedaling.

Soon you come to a gravel road winding down a hill. This time, she goes first as you wait at the top. She glides down like an angel. Now it's your turn. At first it's fine, but you pick up speed, and your bike starts to wobble. You lurch to the other side to compensate, but it's too much, and you wipe out. Hitting the ground, you slide a few feet and then stop. You jump up and wave your arms like you're trying to stop traffic. "I'm alright, I'm alright!"

She runs over like a gazelle and a lifeguard all in one. *Maybe she'll do mouth-to-mouth!* you think. Do gazelles have lips? Lifeguards do. But instead, she asks, "Are you okay?" as she points to the blood running down your leg. And at the hole in her shorts.

"Uhh, sorry about your shorts," you say.

"No problem. You can have 'em."

Now you're thinking it's completely reasonable for her to go home. No one would question her motives should she kindly dismiss herself. No one would think it cruel, no one would judge. All would applaud her. But that's not what she does.

She says, "Let's get a burrito and after that go to Greyhound Rock." So you eat burritos together, borrowing money from her to buy a drink because you only brought ten dollars. And after that, you sit at Greyhound Rock and watch the salt tide roll in and then get ice cream sundaes and meet her friends at the nursing home. It's a long, perfect day.

And even though you have done nothing to impress her or show her that you will treat her like Daddy would want, you're still into each other.

So three months after you meet, you get engaged. When you get married, it's five days short of a year that you first met. The whole thing doesn't make sense, like the way wildflowers grow on a hillside. You don't know how they got there, but you're glad they're there, and you suddenly can't imagine the hillside without them. A hint of red, a dash of purple, a touch of orange; the hillside is better than before.

That's how you feel, that you've marked each other with your brilliant colors, and now you are better than before. All because you biked together and shared a burrito. The common became spectacular, which led to uncommon communion.

Fellowship prayer is spending time with God in an activity that is not traditionally sacred or prayerful. It is casual like friends hanging out together but intentionally sought to build the relationship stronger. You like being together, and your activity draws you closer, although it's not conventionally spiritual. In fellowship prayer, the once-common enterprise becomes holy because God meets you there. It creates uncommon communion.

Genesis 3:8 says, "Then the man and his wife heard the sound of the LORD God as he was walking in the garden in the cool of the day."

The man and his wife were Adam and Eve. Apparently, they knew the sound of God walking in the garden because he had done this before, had come down to them in their garden.

What did it sound like when God came near? Was it loud like mountains crashing, thunder peeling, ground cracking? But God's not always loud. Sometimes he whispers just loud enough to recognize—a butterfly crowning, a breeze blowing, a baby cooing. The Bible doesn't say if God was loud or quiet. But what is certain is that God came down to meet them face-to-face. He had done it before.

She tinkers in her garden. Your first apartment together has no garden, so she builds one. She brings in soil, spreads it out, and then plants lemon verbena so fragrant you'd think you were inside a lemon, red bee balm that looks like little bursting firecrackers, and a rosemary bush with thick, rich tentacles. Your lady waters the garden first, then every day after. She spends a lot of time there, until the day you move into a house and she builds another garden.

She plants sunflowers that tower higher than the children you will raise in that house, red bee balm as a reminder of the days before, and poppies of different shapes and colors. She seems at her best in her garden. She goes there often.

As times goes on, she talks of meeting God in the garden. She explains to you what God has shown her; he has touched her in the garden. She needs to be there. But you don't understand it; to you, gardens are full of weeds to be weeded and holes to be dug and things to be watered. It's full of dirt and worms and trying again when vermin have had their way. Gardens are work.

But not to her.

"Growth is like a garden. God is showing me that," she says, smiling bright as a hyacinth. "Sometimes God turns the soil or waters the weeds, but it's always good. My garden teaches me the seasons of life. God is always at work growing me."

She is radiant with revelation because God has walked in her garden. His presence is there, like when God walked in a garden long ago. How does she grow in God? She meets him in the garden.

But sometimes the voices say this is not the way of spiritual growth. They say she should instead shut herself up in a room, close the windows, shut the blinds. Purge herself of outdoor fantasies, forget frolicking and song, stop playing with dirt and soil. She's an adult now, an adult *Christian* now, time to start acting like one. Time to start praying like one.

Fold your hands, close your eyes, and concentrate really hard. Pray through that list; pray for hours in that hot little room. Make your thous count and your thees plentiful. Crucify the flesh, burn every desire down to the root, rebuke the longing to be outside, to have mud between your fingers and toes. It's time to fellowship with God now.

"But I am praying," she says, "When I'm in my garden, God is with me. I'm becoming a friend of God."

Friendship? What does friendship have to do with God?

Jesus said to his disciples, "I no longer call you servants, because a servant does not know his master's business. Instead I have called you friends, for everything that I learned from my Father I have made known to you" (John 15:15).

They weren't servants anymore; they had become friends. How did they become friends of God? By spending enough time with Jesus that he taught them everything he had learned from his Father. How did they spend enough time with him? By going with Jesus from town to town.

The disciples were around for the big ministry moments—the preaching to the crowds, the healing of infirmities, the raising of the dead. But spending time with Jesus was not all crusades and miracles. It included some very common moments—walking from town to town, eating quiet and lowly meals, the minutes before falling asleep with no place to lay your head. Don't forget that Jesus was human.

Philippians 2:8 says that although Jesus was God, he made himself nothing. For the first time in history, the Son of God, through whom all was made, left his place in heaven. He left the Father and Holy Spirit and went to Earth. And coming to Earth, he was formed in human likeness. He was God but also man.

"And being found in human appearance as a man, he humbled himself and became obedient to death—even death on a cross."

Why did Jesus become human? To satisfy the conditions of judgment. Judgment for sin demanded a perfect man in return. God could not be exchanged for man's sin; a perfect man had to stand in the gap. So Jesus humbled himself in several ways: first by entering earth as a man, second by submitting his life to the will of God, and third by going to the cross.

According to Merriam-Webster's dictionary, the word *humble* comes from a word that means "on the ground." To be humble is to know you're of this earth, formed from dirt and mud. The Son of God became a man; the holy became humble.

Like your lady, your friend wasn't made for the pew. And he's wild too. He's a fly-fisherman.

Casting on the waters to the fish below and to God above, he meets God on the streams and rivers. The empty air and silence and solitude are so full and pregnant that they ring out with the presence of God. On the water, he meets God.

Sure he can be civilized in church. He can dress up and talk nice Christian talk. He can pray, and he can read, and he can even preach. But ask your friend about his best times with God, and he'll say they're not in a building, and they're not in a group. They're not during a service, and they're not reading morning devotions.

His best times with God are fly-fishing (God's a fisher too).

"But I have more important things to do than mess around out there," he sometimes tells himself. "I've got to be a grownup now." Sometimes he feels guilty for not being more religious. Why is he so restless, unable to sit still? Better exorcise the demons. Why does he have to be on the water?

Someone had once told him that patience was a virtue. And he had read in the Bible that God is patient. But it's on the water that he actually learned it. It was the days on the river—the rhythmic casting of the line, the splashing of the fly, the timing he practiced so hard to get right—that finally did it. With rod in hand and feet in the water, he met God on the river. God said to be patient where I have placed you. And when he did, he knew what God was talking about.

And when one day he read that Jesus is the living Water, he knew exactly what Jesus was talking about. He had traversed rushing currents that almost knocked him over. He had waded in gentle eddies that whirled of otherworldly beauty. He had refreshed himself in springs when his day job weighed him down. Water had been living to him in all of life's seasons. Just like Jesus.

But one day, life crashes down on him as life sometimes does. There are no right words that anyone can offer. Bible verses don't comfort and no prayers from people soothe. Not even worship songs lift his heart. So he does what he knows to do to receive from the Lord—he goes fishing. And with each cast and tug of the line, he finds God is there (God can walk on water). And he finds a friend in God, who has been there all along. Fishing helps him see that.

A friend of God knows what God sounds like, quiet or loud. And he goes out to meet him wherever it is. For some it's inside, but for others it's not. For some it's running on the road, soaring in the clouds, deep sea diving. For some it's cooking, making ugly amateur art, attaching electrical circuits, or boating on the lake. Some even garden or fly-fish.

But whatever the holy enterprise is, wherever the common ground may be, the friend of God keeps going there because that is where God walks so you can be together.

Tweets from this Chapter

> » God's not always loud. Sometimes he whispers just loud enough to recognize—a butterfly crowning, a breeze blowing, a baby cooing. @CSHeinz

> » Growth is like a garden. Sometimes God turns the soil or waters or weeds, but it's always good. Gardens teach you seasons of life. @CSHeinz

> » Judgment for sin demanded a perfect man in return. God could not be exchanged for man's sin; a perfect man had to stand in the gap. @CSHeinz

> » A friend of God knows what God sounds like, soft or

loud. And he goes out to meet him, wherever it is. @ CSHeinz

» Fellowship prayer is spending time with God in an activity that is not traditionally sacred or prayerful. @CSHeinz

Discussion Questions

1. What is the definition of fellowship prayer?
2. Has God ever orchestrated something that didn't make any sense at all?
3. Are there any "non-sacred" activities in which you have encountered God?
4. Which type of moment would you have preferred to experience with Jesus—the big moments or the common moments?
5. Can you relate to feeling guilty for not being "religious enough"? Is religious activity the same as heartfelt devotion?
6. Are there areas of your life that the Holy Spirit is weeding and pruning in order to prepare for something to come?
7. When have you experienced Jesus as the living Water?
8. Do you consider yourself a friend of God? Why or why not?
9. Is there anything holding you back from deepening your friendship with God?
10. Do you feel drawn to this type of prayer?

7
Warfare Prayer

In order to take the Gospel to every creature, the
Church is called to engage the forces of evil.
—Ed Silvoso, *That None Should Perish*[16]

For our struggle is not against flesh and blood, but
against the rulers, against the authorities, against
the powers of this dark world and against the
spiritual forces of evil in the heavenly realms.
—Ephesians 6:12

Definition of Warfare Prayer: Confronting the kingdom of Satan
with the weapons of God's kingdom

Bible Characters: The Seventy-two Others

"**H**EY, DO YOU WANT TO preach in my place?" your friend
asks. He's supposed to preach at church on Sunday, but

now he can't. He offers the spot to you. *How hard can it be?* you think. You accept.

The sermon goes well. You preach on holiness. The attendees nod and say "amen" in agreement. Everyone is happy, and afterward you offer to pray for them.

The people who want prayer line up in the front. You begin to go down the rows, pausing at each person to pray. You can hear the Holy Spirit. You pass on words and remind them of promises and agree for breakthroughs. It's easy to operate in this flow.

Until you get to her. As you pray for a particular woman, she starts coughing. It's not a singular cough to clear the airway, but a coughing fit. You wonder if she might clear a lung. You take a step back. Then she begins dry heaving. You wonder if she'll vomit. You take another step back. You like your shoes. At this point, everyone looks at you. What will you do about it?

What will I do about it? She's in your church. What will you *do about it? I'm just the guest preacher.*

But then a statement pops into your mind. "In my name, they will drive out demons." Demons? You haven't had much experience with demons—that you know of. But currently you notice a certain fragrance of evil, chaos, and unrest, a very present darkness drawing attention to itself. Its origin is unknown, but its effects are remarkable. Peace has left the building, and everyone is staring up front. The statement returns to you, "In my name, they will drive out demons."

So you gird up, straighten your shoulders, and tell the demon to leave in Jesus' name.

And you know what? It does. The chaos clears, the woman settles, and peace returns to the room. The people start praising God. You thank God for helping you out.

But you feel disturbed. God came through this time, but what about the next time? Will there be a next time? What just happened exactly? Why didn't you know what to do? And why didn't they?

A few years later, you're discussing this experience with a friend. You ask, "Have you experienced much spiritual warfare?"

She says, "No, I've been lucky. I haven't faced much warfare at all."

But you've been learning. You look into her eyes and say, "Perhaps avoiding spiritual warfare isn't the point."

She darts her eyes from yours, grabs her Cosmo, and takes a sip, "Whatever."

Ephesians 6:12 says, "For our struggle is not against flesh and blood, but against the rulers, against the authorities, against the powers of this dark world and against the spiritual forces of evil in the heavenly realms."

Warfare prayer is confronting the kingdom of Satan with the weapons of God's kingdom. God's kingdom includes God the Father, the Son, and the Holy Spirit, angels and angelic authorities, God's word that is living and active, faith that is a substance, spiritual weapons, people who serve the living God, and manifestations of their work.

On the other hand, Satan's kingdom includes Satan himself, his spiritual forces, people who serve the Devil, and the manifestations of their work, including strongholds, falsehoods, temptations, and ungodly bonds.

You were born into the conflict between God and Satan, so expect war. In the beginning of the world, God created angels—spiritual beings whose job is to serve God. There was one particular angel called "Morning Star" and "Son of the Dawn." Higher than the other angels, he was an archangel. But he longed for more. He wanted the glory and honor for himself, so he turned against God. Satan started a rebellion with one-third of the angels. Thus began the war.

This conflict is spiritual, but it manifests in the natural world. After the Devil lost his place in heaven, he was hurled to the earth with the members of his kingdom. They were sent to the world of men, to your rolling hills and steeping mountains, your quiet brooks and dense forests. They came to your cities and farms, to your families and marriages. They invaded humanity.

And they hate you.

They hate you because they hate God. They hate you because God made you for himself. They hate you because you have the choice to follow God. That's precisely where Satan attacks—at your God-given choice of whom to follow. God wants you to follow him so you'll have abundant life. Satan doesn't. Like all wars, it's a matter of life and death.

You've had this nagging feeling that there's more going on. Life is more than doing the laundry and earning a paycheck, meeting a nice someone, having some kids, retiring, and then dying. There's more out there, like if you could slice the atmosphere and look inside, you would see many comings and goings, celestial battles, words throbbing with life, forces coming to your aid. You'd see what is more real than your earth, what existed long before you did, and what will persist after you leave this rock.

Before Jesus was born, it was prophesied that he would set the captives free—he would release the oppressed and proclaim the Lord's favor (this is war language). When Jesus was born, Satan tried to snuff out the newborn Messiah, killing all the infant boys in the land. But he didn't succeed in killing Jesus.

At the start of Jesus' ministry, he faced the Devil in the desert, where the Devil tempted him with visions of rule, comfort, and stability. But Jesus overcame the attacks of the Enemy. This set the paradigm for the rest of his ministry—it would be war, but Jesus would overcome.

When Jesus entered a town, it was common for the people to

bring the demon-possessed to him, and Jesus would heal them. He fulfilled his destiny to set the captives free. Along the way, he picked up the twelve disciples, who traveled with him all the time. They witnessed firsthand Jesus' encounters with the dark powers and his confrontations with the dark kingdom. Then Jesus gave them the authority to do the same. They went from being spectators to warriors themselves.

But the power sharing didn't end there. After sending out the twelve disciples, Jesus appointed seventy-two others to go ahead of him to the towns and villages where they would minister to the people and prepare their hearts to receive Jesus. The seventy-two others were to do four things:

» Bless the houscholds

» Fellowship with the people

» Cast out demons and heal the sick (some sicknesses are caused by demons)

» Say the kingdom of God has come near

The result? "The seventy-two returned with joy and said, 'Lord, even the demons submit to us in your name,'" (Luke 10:17).

But the power sharing didn't end there either. The last words Jesus said before ascending to heaven were to make disciples and drive out demons, "Go into all the world and preach the good news to all creation. Whoever believes and is baptized will be saved, but whoever does not believe will be condemned. And these signs will accompany those who believe: In my name they will drive out demons" (Mark 16:15–17).

Jesus was not talking to himself or the twelve or the seventy-two; he was talking to you. According to the Anchor Bible Dictionary, the term *Christian* means, "a follower of Christ." The purpose of Christianity is to produce people who follow Christ. Jesus instructs you to make followers, but that's only part of it. He also wants you to confront the kingdom of Satan. Warfare prayer prepares the climate for Jesus.

In C. S. Lewis's classic book, *The Lion, the Witch and the Wardrobe*, Peter, Edmund, Susan, and Lucy become kings and queens of Narnia after they defeat the White Witch, who has usurped the throne. Although the White Witch has many dreadful creatures on her side, the children have many valiant creatures on theirs, including Aslan, the mighty king of the whole forest.

In the end, the children win the war and claim their thrones. But that doesn't mean they retire to Palm Springs to play golf.

Lewis writes,

> These two Kings and two Queens governed Narnia well, and long and happy was their reign. At first much of their time was spent in seeking out the remnants of the White Witch's army and destroying them, and indeed for a long time there would be news of evil things lurking in the wilder parts of the forest—a haunting here and a killing there, a glimpse of a werewolf one month and a rumor of a hag the next.[17]

Satan is a loser because, well, he lost. Jesus won the war because he disarmed the powers and authorities and made a public spectacle of them. But that doesn't mean all is well. There is still evil lurking about. The choice is given to every man and woman—who will they follow? The battle rages on for the souls of men. Will you fight for them? Will you enter spiritual warfare for their sake?

First Corinthians 10:3-4 says, "For though we live in the world, we do not wage war as the world does. The weapons we fight with are not the weapons of the world." Warfare prayer is taking up your spiritual weapons and confronting the Enemy. To use your weapons, you have to know what they are.

Here are ten of them:

Holy Spirit

Sometimes the Holy Spirit leads you into battle to overcome the Enemy. The Holy Spirit isn't interested in your being comfortable. His goal is not to provide you with a life of endless room service and in-room movies, full-body massages, and terry cloth bathrobes.

Matthew 4:1 says, "Then Jesus was led by the Spirit into the desert to be tempted by the devil." There are two uncomfortable truths here. First, the Holy Spirit led Jesus into the desert. The desert was not the Hyatt; it was full of wild animals, shelter-less days and nights, the beating sun, and no food or water. And Jesus was alone. Second, the Holy Spirit led Jesus there to be tempted by the Devil. Not only was his setting completely miserable, but Jesus was attacked as well. The Holy Spirit led Jesus there on purpose.

But if there's no attack, there's no victory. God wanted to make a statement as Jesus headed into public ministry—it would be war, but Jesus would overcome. So don't be surprised if the Holy Spirit leads you into battle. Rather than your comfort or happiness, the Holy Spirit is fixed on bringing glory to God. And sometimes that glory is gained from battle. But take heart. The Holy Spirit is with you.

Blood of Jesus

The blood of Jesus is the most powerful substance in the universe because it liberates you from death when you receive it.

This blood creates right standing before God and makes sons and daughters of God. How precious is this blood that was spilled on your account! Once you receive the work of the blood, you are under the blood.

A friend nervously awaits results from her blood work. She has suffered from fears and anxieties while waiting for the numbers. They could change her life; her future is thrown into a fog. She can't sleep, can't sit still. A feeling of dread envelops her. But the blood work has already been done, you say to her. She is covered.

Such protection this blood affords you! You have been forgiven by God. Your position as a child of God is secure. You walk in fellowship with the Holy Spirit. You belong to God and possess every spiritual blessing. The Devil has no right to you.

But sometimes he tries to weasel his way in. The work of Satan is to undermine the blood of Jesus. He tempts you and taunts you to doubt your salvation. He wants you to think the blood isn't as strong as you think; that it's watered down, weak. But in warfare prayer, you stand beneath the blood of Jesus and proclaim its benefits. You declare that the Enemy has no authority over those who are blood-bought.

Name of Jesus

If the blood of Jesus is the most powerful substance ever, the name of Jesus is the most powerful name. At the name of Jesus every knee shall bow. At the name of Jesus everyone will say who they think he is. The name of Jesus turns you into a spiritual warrior. When you bear the name of Jesus, it's a sign of your relationship with him and the authority granted you.

Authority is the power to command. Jesus deputizes you through his name. In warfare prayer, you exercise the authority of Jesus over the Enemy, who operates by intimidation. He'll try to frighten you with fantasies because he knows there is no greater name than Jesus. And he'll tempt you to belittle your authority so you get out of the way.

You'll think, *Little ol' me. How can I fight such a force?* But "follower of Christ" does not mean being impotent, scrawny, or amateur. It means being shaped and formed and connected to the original. So pray often in Jesus' name. Cast out demons in Jesus' name. Declare the victory in Jesus' name. There's certainly no more powerful or sweeter name.

Truth of God

Another way the Enemy operates is through lies. In fact, he's called the Father of Lies. Much spiritual battle occurs in the mind. He'll twist your beliefs from the truth of God or grow falsehood in your understanding. Unless you regularly feast on the truth of God, you will not recognize when the root of deception is taking hold.

He'll tempt you to make ungodly vows or bonds. A vow is a binding promise or agreement you make to another party. An ungodly bond is a connection with another person that can result from legitimate disappointments, like when a father leaves his family, for example. His daughter might make a vow never to trust men because she believes that no men are trustworthy. And since she can't trust her father, she can't trust God, her heavenly Father. She has made a vow. But what's the truth? Just because one man—albeit an important man—abandoned her, it doesn't mean all men will. And it doesn't mean God will. Unless she bases her life on God's truth, the Enemy will use her experiences to reinforce false beliefs.

But 2 Corinthians 10:5 says, "We demolish arguments and every pretension that sets itself up against the knowledge of God, and we take captive every thought to make it obedient to Christ." A pretension is an allegation of doubtful value. The Enemy is called the Accuser, and his allegations have no value. In warfare prayer, the spiritual warrior destroys every argument and pretension that opposes the knowledge of God. He is an expert at detecting falsehood like a hound hunting a fox.

Armor of God

One morning you're getting ready for work, and you slide on an undershirt. It feels tight and uncomfortable, but you're in a hurry, so you put a polo shirt on top and go to work. During the day, the undershirt keeps riding up your stomach and squeezing your sides. You don't like it at all. Later at home, you tell your wife how she ruined your day because she shrunk your shirt in the laundry.

She says she could stop doing your laundry. You say, "Never mind then. Forget about it."

Then she asks to see your shirt, so you lift up your polo shirt. She hits the ground, laughing.

"This is hardly a time to laugh," you say, all cranky and disturbed.

She chortles louder. "That's *my* shirt! No wonder it doesn't fit!"

Your wife's shirt might not fit you, but the armor of God always does. Ephesians 6:13 says, "Therefore put on the full armor of God, so that when the day of evil comes, you may be able to stand your ground, and after you have done everything, to stand."

The armor of God is God's gift to you comprised of weapons of offense, defense, and stability:

- » Belt of Truth
- » Breastplate of Righteousness

» Shoes of the Gospel of Peace

» Shield of Faith

» Helmet of Salvation

» Sword of the Spirit

The armor of God reminds you that God has equipped you for battle.

When you pray, you put on the full armor of God. Imagine yourself saddling up your gear: you lace up your shoes, praying for the gospel to penetrate unbelievers; you fasten your belt, girded by God's word; you position the breastplate, covered by Christ; you slide on your helmet, secure in your salvation; you grasp your shield, protected by God's pleasure; and you take up your sword, which divides the heart. You are God's warrior, armed and ready.

Angels

One underutilized weapon in God's kingdom is your accessibility to angels, but you can ask God to send angels to help you. Hebrews 1:14 says that angels are ministering spirits sent to members of God's kingdom. But they're underused.

Angels are in need of a public-image makeover. The popular view on angels is that they're chubby babies in cloth diapers, flittering with tiny wings, carrying miniature harps and bows and arrows, and shooting sweethearts so they fall in love. The best an angel can achieve is a wedding between sweethearts. With this picture of angels, it's not surprising you don't call on them to help. When under attack, you need a warrior, not a baby going wee-wee. You need a ninja, not a nookie.

But here's what angels have really done:

» Wrestled with Satan and thrown him to the earth

» Fought with Jacob until morning

» Tended to Jesus after he was tempted by Satan in the desert

» Killed the firstborn sons of the Egyptians

» Proclaimed messages from God

» Struck Herod, killing him

» Helped Peter escape from prison

» Guided the Israelites to the Promised Land

» Continues to guard and protect you

But between angels and demons, angels tend to get less attention. Perhaps because the Enemy operates by fear and intimidation, his forces feel stronger and infinite. But remember that when Satan rebelled against God, he took only one-third of the angels with him. That left two-thirds of them with God. So for every demonic spirit, there are two godly angels. Angels outnumber demons two to one. The odds are in your favor.

After the seventy-two others returned from warfare praying, they marveled that the demons submitted to them. But Jesus corrected them by saying, "Do not rejoice that the spirits submit to you, but rejoice that your names are written in heaven" (Luke 10:20). That is, focus on God's kingdom, not the spirits. Still, it's wise to understand the Enemy's kingdom so you know how to fight.

» There are three levels of spiritual warfare: ground-level, occult-level, and strategic-level.[18]

» Ground-level spiritual warfare deals with demons. Demons are the most common enemy found in the New Testament. They're also called evil spirits and unclean spirits.

» Demons can speak, have feelings, and are assigned specific tasks.

» Demons can have superhuman strength although they don't have physical bodies of their own.

» Demons can cause sicknesses, emotional disturbances, relational troubles, and more.

» Occult-level spiritual warfare is empowered and released through witchcraft.

» The work of occult-level spiritual beings is more catastrophic than the work of demons.

» Strategic-level spiritual warfare involves powers that influence geographical territories.

» Territorial powers can hold entire regions in bondage.

In warfare prayer, you become a friend to angels, asking God to release them on your behalf. They're eager to fight for you and rout some demons. So take them out of time-out.

Fasting

In Matthew 17, a father is desperate. His son often has seizures and falls into the fire. The disciples have tried to help him but without success. Now the father asks Jesus to step in. Jesus agrees, rebukes the demon, and it comes out of the boy. Why did Jesus succeed when his disciples failed?

Jesus explains, "This kind does not go out except by prayer and fasting" (v. 20).

When Jesus first teaches on fasting, he says, "*When* you fast," not, "*If* you fast." To Jesus, fasting is a regular and necessary practice. Prayer by itself isn't enough to heal the boy, but fasting provides the extra edge to overcome the Enemy. Fasting heightens your spiritual authority and increases your spiritual vision.

In fasting, you abstain from natural provisions and focus on spiritual provisions. In fasting, you go without your natural comforts, fallbacks, and routines so God becomes your one and only, which bonds you with him. With fasting, you have more time for prayer. You realize this world is not your own. You are separated for God, a citizen of heaven. You are not ruled by your appetites and cravings; you are self-controlled and your mind is ready for action. When you fast, you are more sensitive to God's voice and discerning truth.

Forgiveness

Forgiveness is a supernatural act that closes the door to demonic entry. Satan's kingdom is legalistic; he looks for any right to remain. Unforgiveness and bitterness leave the door open, but forgiveness removes the right. It announces, "No vacancy!"

According to Vine's Dictionary, to forgive means "to send forth, to send away." In forgiveness, you send the offense away. As soon as someone sins against you, a debt is created on your relational account. Sending the offense away is necessary to keep a short account between each other. It also keeps a short account between you and God. Jesus said if you don't forgive people of their sins, then God won't forgive your sins (Matthew 6:15).

Forgiveness is not forgetting. The offense is sent away but not necessarily the memory. You might still remember what happened, and in some cases, you need to remember. But just because you haven't forgotten doesn't mean you haven't forgiven.

Also, forgiveness is not living like the offense never happened. In fact, it's living with the consequences of the offense. Certain offenses will necessitate change. If you have to modify the relationship—introduce boundaries or regain trust—it doesn't mean you haven't forgiven. It means you're living with the consequences. The spiritual warrior confesses his sin and forgives others.

Praise

Revelation 12:11 says, "They overcame [Satan] by the blood of the Lamb and by the word of their testimony." When you announce what God has done, it releases praise. The Devil hates praise; it's the reason he turned from God in the first place. When you begin to testify about God's work in your life, you change the spiritual climate.

All hell may be breaking loose around you, but your testimony fixes you firmly on God. It also lifts others to see what God can do. Praise moves the focus from the Enemy to God. When you say what God has done, it restores confidence that God will come through. And it teaches the Enemy a lesson: When he attacks you, you praise God, which is something he doesn't want.

Be like Paul and Silas. They were attacked by a crowd, stripped and beaten, and then thrown into prison with their feet in stocks. But rather than pitying themselves or being mad at God or withdrawing into themselves, they praised God instead. They overcame their feelings and testified about God's goodness. As a result, a violent earthquake shook the prison and released them from their cells and chains (Acts 16:25).

Blessing

When Jesus sent out the seventy-two others, the first thing he instructed them to do was bless the household, as this would introduce the kingdom of God. Although it seems passive, blessing is a powerful spiritual weapon. Blessing is the opposite spirit of how the Enemy operates. "The tongue has the power of life and death," says Proverbs 18:21.

To bless is to speak well of people or request divine care for them. It's to ask God to do good for others before he does good for you. Blessing is especially potent when the Enemy has enlisted someone to come against you. This war is not against flesh and blood, but Satan uses people for his purposes. In warfare prayer, you love your enemies. You pray blessing over them and ask God to protect their hearts and minds. You do nice things for them. You startle them with love.

It's easy to curse when you're being cursed, to criticize when you're being criticized. But blessing is not just turning the other cheek; it's offering your cloak in return. Blessing is combatting death with life. You may not see the results of blessing immediately, but be assured that blessing is doing a good work.

So take up the mighty weapons of your warfare. God gave them so you would use them valiantly, not store them in your closet.

Your friend calls you; she'd like to get together. But not for the usual Cosmos. This time she'd like a private place to pray with you. *This is most unusual,* you think. She'll be right over.

"I've been doing a lot of thinking," she says.

"Well, that's a change," as you nudge her shoulder.

"Seriously, what you said really affected me. I've been trying to avoid spiritual warfare. I've let others press into God. I've let others fight my battles. But I've realized no one can walk my walk with God and no one can win my battles except me. It's time I take my place. Will you teach me to fight?"

And from that day forth, she becomes a very fierce warrior, one of God's most chosen, and when he must send someone, he sends her, because she is a fighter God can bank on.

Tweets from this Chapter

» You were born into the conflict between God and Satan. The conflict is spiritual, but it manifests on the earth. @ CSHeinz

» God wants you to follow him so you'll have abundant

life. Satan doesn't. Like all wars it's a matter of life and death. @CSHeinz

» The term "Christian" means follower of Christ. The purpose of Christianity is to produce people who follow Christ. @CSHeinz

» Satan is a loser because well, he lost. Jesus disarmed the powers and authorities and made a public spectacle of them (Col 2:15). @CSHeinz

» Sometimes the Holy Spirit leads you to battle to overcome the enemy. The Holy Spirit isn't interested in keeping you comfortable. @CSHeinz

» The blood of Jesus is the most powerful substance in the universe because it liberates you from death when you receive it. @CSHeinz

» One underutilized weapon in God's kingdom is your accessibility to angels, but you can ask God to send angels to help you. @CSHeinz

» In fasting, you go without your natural comforts, fallbacks, and routines, so God becomes your one and only. @CSHeinz

» Forgiveness is a supernatural act that closes the door to demonic entry. @CSHeinz

Discussion Questions

1. What is the definition of spiritual warfare?
2. Have you ever sensed the demonic realm?
3. What are some examples from Jesus' life of facing the kingdom of darkness?
4. When has the Holy Spirit led you into battle?

5. What four things did Jesus tell the seventy-two others to do?

6. Of the ten spiritual weapons discussed, which ones do you favor?

7. Who is someone you can bless in order to change the spiritual climate?

8. What is the most powerful substance in the universe? Why?

9. How often do you ask for angelic help?

10. Do you feel drawn to this type of prayer?

8
Praying the Bible

The Bible is a ready-made prayer book for God's family.
We "pray the Bible" when we use passages of Scripture
to form prayers, or when we say the verses directly
back to God, making them our own petitions.
—David Kopp, *Praying the Bible for Your Life*[19]

Do not let the Book of the Law depart from
your mouth; meditate on it day and night.
—Joshua 1:8

Definition of Praying the Bible: Praying the words of the Bible
as your prayer

Bible Character: Joshua

Y OU LISTEN TO AN INTERVIEW on the radio. A woman in her
twenties is driving when, all of a sudden, she swerves to avoid

an obstruction in the road and hits a tree head-on. Metal collides with bark. The metal on the car crumbles; the flesh crumbles inside. The car catches fire, but the woman is pinned down and cannot escape.

Help arrives. They rip her from the burning car, but her injuries are substantial. Cars aren't supposed to hit trees, people aren't supposed to be in cars that hit trees. The help says she probably won't make it to the hospital alive. That's when she phones her mom from the back of the ambulance. She can barely talk.

But Mom can barely talk too. Getting a call like this leaves you speechless as a parent. And that's what it does. But her daughter needs her. Mom tries to regain her composure, get her footing, and do what needs to be done. That's what moms do in a crisis. She scans for a moment and then grabs onto words she has learned, ancient words from the Holy Book.

She prays, "God, you know the plans you have for her" (she's remembering Jeremiah 29:11). New tears fill her eyes, and her throat tightens. A picture of her daughter in pigtails flashes through her mind, her high school graduation gown, her dimples. She thinks about stopping, but she must keep going. "God, they're plans to prosper her and not to harm her, plans to give her a hope and a future."

She prays it again, straightening her shoulders, firming her voice, "God, you know the plans you have for her, plans to prosper her and not to harm her, plans to give her a hope and a future." Over and over she prays the ancient words that are alive until she must hang up because the ambulance has arrived at the hospital and, with it, her very much alive daughter. It's contrary to what the help said.

Not only that, the daughter is soon healed of her injuries. Yes, the effects of the bone-crushing, flesh-crumbling accident are gone. And because of all this, the attending doctor who doesn't believe in God begins to. Life springs up where it wasn't expected.

God gave the mom his words when she didn't have her own. God gives his words to you too.

Praying the Bible is praying the words of the Bible as your prayer. God's words become the content of your conversation with him. You say his words back to him, and as you do, you tap into the ancient words that are alive. And when you do, you connect with the generations before you who prayed God's Word.

You pray like Joshua. Joshua was the leader who took over for Moses on the Israelite's forty-year exodus out of slavery and into destiny. The former slaves were on their way to the Promised Land. Before Moses died, he appointed Joshua as the new leader to guide the million or so people to their inheritance. This was no easy task, so young Joshua depended on God's guidance.

What did God say as he passed the baton? His advice is very interesting. I mean, a million people walking in the desert, a million who are prone to grumbling and idolatry, who at times want to go back to slavery. God, please say something good because Joshua needs you.

So God advised Joshua to keep God's Word on his lips and to meditate on it day and night. Joshua was to keep God's Word always in front of him. This would be the key to entering the Promised Land and receiving the inheritance. But this is very interesting because you think meditation is a passive activity. How will meditation deliver these people to their destination?

You think of yoga mats and humming, bamboo and silence. You think of bonsai trees and folded legs. You think of emptying yourself of everything. But this isn't what God is talking about. Meditating on God's Word is not an emptying but a filling of the timeless wisdom of God. When you meditate on God, you are filled.

When God told Joshua to meditate on his Word, he used the word *hagah*, which means to "growl, utter, speak."[20] This word is actually used of lions who growl and birds who sing. There's nothing silent about meditation. And why would there be? Joshua was a leader and a warrior, tough enough to command a million. The first time you meet Joshua is in Exodus 17 when Moses told him to take men and fight the Amalekites.

And the result? Verse 17 says, "So Joshua overcame the Amalekite army with the sword." Pay attention to the particular detail of the sword because it is important—Joshua overcame the enemy *with the sword*. Then you remember that as God appointed Joshua as successor, he instructed Joshua to meditate on his Word day and night. And then it hits you—Ephesians calls the Word of God *"the sword of the Spirit,"* and Hebrews says the Word of God is sharper than *"any two-edged sword."* So Joshua overcame them *with the sword*.

There's something to these sword references. Meditating on God's Word is the way Joshua will lead the Israelites to their inheritance. The path to the Promised Land is paved with the ancient words.

This reminds you of your forefathers, the Jews. Ever since they received the Word of God, they built their lives around it. When you pray the Bible, you join in an activity practiced by generations before you.

Praying the Bible connects you to your roots. Every morning, the Jews prayed a prayer called the Shema:

> Hear, O Israel: The LORD our God, the LORD is one. Love the LORD your God with all your heart and with all your strength. These commandments that I give you today are to be upon your hearts. Impress them on your children. Talk about them when you sit at home and when you walk along

the road, when you lie down and when you get
up (Deuteronomy 6:4–7).

The Shema wasn't just a prayer; it was a way of life. When
your forefathers awoke, they meditated on God's Word, and
when they went to bed, they did the same. When they walked
upon the road and sat at home in the evening, they talked about
it. God's Word was the center of their lives. They were people
of the Book.

The members of the early church were too. Composed
primarily of Jews, they prayed Scripture when they gathered
and when they were alone. On the day of Pentecost, they were
together in one place. They came to pray, to speak the ancient
words in and out to God and to each other. Their Jesus had
been crucified so what else did they have? Suddenly, there was
a rushing wind, the promised Holy Spirit, and they devoted
themselves even more to prayer.

Jesus was a man of the Book too. Raised a Jew, Jesus would
have prayed the Shema daily. He would have been taught about
his forefather Joshua, the meditation honored, the inheritance
received. And when Jesus was tempted by the Devil in the
wilderness, he responded with God's Word. This was the key
to his resistance. When Jesus taught the crowds about God, he
quoted God's Word. It was the key to his revelation.

Praying the Bible also helps you memorize Scripture. You think
of the useless facts that are wedged in your mind, such as your
childhood phone number and RBI stats of a player long gone.
You spin off the chorus of a song you don't care about and the
address of your first loser boyfriend. But you can't memorize the
Bible to win a game show, even though you're supposed to be a
person of the Book.

Praying the Bible will help. Usually when you have tried to
memorize Scripture, you've tried to do it with your mind. You

repeated a few words, attempted to keep them in the correct order, and then repeated the next phrase, and so forth. But when you pray the Bible, your spirit gets involved.

The eternal in you interacts with the eternal of God's Word, the ancient words that are alive, and a spiritual transaction occurs. Suddenly, your true essence, your spirit, connects with the Holy Word, and spirit power is produced. Spirit power always trumps mind power when you pray the Bible.

Praying the Bible fixes your mind on God. The mind can be a hapless organ. You tell it what to do, but it doesn't listen. It wanders off. Soon it's hunting for honeycombs and butterflies. You guide it back to the trail. But it's not long before it's chasing dragonflies and yellowtails and heading toward the dragon even though you gave specific directions not to.

So you scurry after it and right its way. This can be utterly exhausting, but praying the Bible helps to keep your mind on track.

When you pray the Bible, you pray God's will. Do you always know what to pray? Of course you don't. God's will isn't fickle, but it's not always easy to find. So where do you find it? In God's Word. This is to say, God's Word reveals God's will. If you want to know God's will, get to know God's Word, and if you want to pray God's will, then pray God's Word.

You can see why praying God's Word helped Joshua bring the million into the Promised Land and how it enabled Jesus to remain faithful. You can see how it tied the Jews together and empowered the early church into world-changing ministry. Praying the Bible activated their spirits, focused them on God, and enabled them to pray God's will.

You want the same for yourself, would like some spiritual power, please, so you decide to try it. It's such a different way of praying than you've learned, but you're after something different.

You're after your inheritance, receiving every promise God has promised you. You're after your destiny—fulfilling every calling God has given you. You're after a noble mind and an obedient life, the will of God.

Here are four ways to pray the Bible:

» Meditating on it

» Making it personal

» Mashing up Bible prayers

» Moving through a list

To mediate on the Bible, first choose a section of Scripture and then turn your thoughts to God. Begin reading slowly, out loud. Others have called this pray-reading. Pay attention to the words that stick out, screaming for you to pick them, so you do.

Pause at those words that blink like neon signs and let them work. The living Word of God surges in your spirit. You hover over them and wait to see what happens. You might see an image or settle on a thought. You might hear God speaking to your heart. When you feel released from each situation, move on. But not until then. Don't concern yourself with speed or completion of the passage.

For example, you choose Psalm 34:18, which says, "The LORD is close to the brokenhearted and saves those who are crushed in spirit." You pray, "Lord, you are close to the brokenhearted."

You stop at the word *brokenhearted*, remembering times when you were brokenhearted. This causes you to cry out and ask for God's comfort for the brokenhearted because you needed his comfort when you were brokenhearted. And so do they.

And you remember that the heart is the wellspring of life, and so you ask God to heal the brokenhearted because a broken heart is hard to live with. You might even see a picture of a shattered heart in your mind and God putting it back together again. So you agree with God to restore broken lives. Hence, your meditation becomes an experience with God over the word *brokenhearted*.

You can also pray the Bible by making it personal. The Bible is, after all, God's Word to you. Simply insert, "God, you said," into verses that contain God's commands or promises, replacing the pronouns to make it work. For example: "You shall have no other gods before me" (Exodus 20:3). You make it personal by praying, "*God, you said* to have no other gods before you."

Or "The LORD your God is with you, he is mighty to save" (Zephaniah 3:17). You make it personal by praying, "*God, you said* that you are with me and are mighty to save."

You also insert the name of a person into a verse, such as John 3:1, which says, "How great is the love the Father has lavished on us, that we should be called children of God!" To pray this verse for your friend Marcus Petarkus, you pray, "How great is the love the Father has lavished on *Marcus*, that *Marcus* should be called a child of God!"

You like this so far, so you do more. *You create a Bible mash-up prayer.* A song mash-up is a combination of songs that are laid seamlessly back-to-back. You can do the same with Bible verses. Instead of praying one passage, stitch together related Bible verses to form a Bible mash-up prayer.

Pick a topic, say humility, and string together verses about humility. "God, you ask why do we look at the speck in our brother's eye and pay no attention to the plank in our own eye? You ask why do we look down on our brother? We know that when we judge others, we will be judged with the same measure we use. We will all stand before your seat in judgment. God, you oppose the proud but give grace to the humble. Convict us of our pride, Lord, and lead us to humility" (Matthew 7:2–3; Romans 14:10; James 4:6).

Or marriage: "God, you say that a man will leave his father and mother and be united with his wife. You say that he who finds a wife finds a good thing. Surely a wife is a lily among the thorns, and a husband is an apple tree among the trees of the forest. They will become one, apple tree and lily, husband and wife. A cord of three is not easily broken—the husband, the wife, and Christ" (Ephesians 5:31–32; Proverbs 18:22; Song of Songs 2:2–3; Ecclesiastes 4:12).

Another way to pray the Bible is to move through a list. You have a shopping list, a bucket list, a birthday list, and a "honey do" list, so what's another list? But this one helps you pray the Word of God. You make a list of the names of Jesus in the Bible, such as:

> » Bread of Life (John 6:33)
>
> » Chief Shepherd (1 Peter 5:4)
>
> » Head of the Church (Ephesians 1:22)

You pray the list, saying, "Jesus, you're the bread of life. You sustain me and fill my hunger. You are tasty to my soul and have risen."

Or "Jesus, you're the chief shepherd. You go after the single sheep who has gone astray. You lead me to quiet pastures. I hear your voice and trust you."

Or you may make a list of the characteristics of God:

> » Wise (Romans 11:33)
>
> » Holy (Leviticus 11:44)
>
> » Faithful (1 Corinthians 10:13)

Then you pray, "God, you are wise. You know what you're doing. You teach me in the right time and answer my prayers perfectly."

Or "God, you're holy. There is no one like you. You are pure and lifted up."

Another type of list is composed of identity statements directly from Scripture, describing who you are in Christ. You think this would benefit you because you're not sure who you are. You've let others define you, but now you want God to define you. You want to know what God thinks of you so you can live by his definition.

> » I am God's child (John 1:12)
> » I am God's agent (2 Corinthians 6:1)
> » I am a friend of God (John 15:15)

You pray, "God, I'm your child. You knit me together in my mother's womb. You have a plan and want the best for me. You're my father and lavish your love on me."

Or "God, I'm your agent. You have invited me to partner with you to expand your kingdom. Use me to accomplish your will. Empower me to do great works."

So you try out the ancient words in prayer, and as you do, you feel the mantle of Joshua. You see him standing before the masses and the enemies, facing the journey ahead. The living words are on his lips and on your lips, and you both overcome.

When you pray the Bible, you grip the sword that divides soul and spirit. It's heavy in your hand because it contains eternity. You sense the spiritual lives of your forefathers who uttered and growled and spoke the living words. They gathered, dispersed, and then came back together. The breath between them was the air of the ancient and alive. And as you pray that way, new life pulses within you. Life springs up where it isn't expected.

Tweets from this Chapter

» Praying the Bible is praying the words of the Bible as your prayer. @CSHeinz

» Meditating on God's Word is not an emptying, but a filling of the timeless wisdom of God. When you meditate on God, you are filled. @CSHeinz

» When you pray the Bible, you join in an activity practiced by generations before you. It connects you to your roots. @CSHeinz

» Here are four ways to pray the Bible: meditating on it, making it personal, mashing up Bible prayers, and moving through a list. @CSHeinz

» If you want to know God's will, then get to know God's Word, and if you want to pray God's will, then pray God's Word. @CSHeinz

» Praying the Bible fixes your mind on God. The mind can be a hapless organ. You tell it what to do, but it doesn't listen. @CSHeinz

» When you pray the Bible, you grip the sword that divides soul and spirit. @CSHeinz

Discussion Questions

1. Have you ever prayed the Bible or is this new to you?
2. Have you ever been in a situation when you didn't know what to pray? How would praying the Bible have helped you?
3. How is the church the people of the Word?
4. How is the Bible the sword of the Spirit?

5. When you read the Bible, do you allow for the Holy Spirit to hover?

6. What are some benefits of praying the Bible?

7. What are some ways to pray Scripture?

8. Think of a dilemma that someone is facing. What Scriptures can you pray?

9. What is a Bible mash-up prayer? For what topic would you like to create one now?

10. Do you feel drawn to this prayer type?

Prayer of Confession

You and I are not alone in our constant struggle to ward off sin and temptation and fight its lingering effects. Until we own that and stop parading around as if perfect, there will be very little power of God manifested in our lives.
—Dannah Gresh, *The Secret of the Lord*[21]

Wash me clean from my guilt. Purify me from my sin. For I recognize my rebellion; it haunts me day and night.
—Psalm 51:2–3, NLT

Definition of Prayer of Confession: Acknowledging your sin to God and then celebrating the forgiveness you have received

Bible Character: David

LET'S SAY YOU'RE A BOY, and your family has moved into a new house. You and your brothers find adventures around every corner. A big green bush sits between your house and the house next door. You figure out you can ring the doorbell and dash behind the bush with just enough time to hide yourself. Then crouching, you watch the neighbor open the door to find no one there. It's hilarious. You cup your mouths to hide your laughter. This never gets old.

The house also has an attic, which rises to unbearable temperatures during the summer. You crawl inside, shut the door, and begin sweltering immediately. You dare each other to go farther in. The farther in, the hotter it is and the longer it will take to get out. Who will last the longest before sprinting to the door? Beads of sweat turn into streams, salt seeps into your eyes. You're in the Sahara Desert, pretending to be men.

But the best part of the house is the basement. It's partially finished with a concrete floor and is framed out with wooden studs. Someday it will be civilized, turned into a bedroom, painted a safe-housewife beige or tan. Neutral carpet will be laid down and oak furniture placed on top, maybe a fake plant or two. But not yet. For now, it's your fort.

You outfit your fort with the necessary equipment. Who knows how long you'll be stopped up inside? You bring in food rations (Twinkies), extra clothes (Superman pajamas), and bedding (GI Joe sleeping bags). You even bring in a toilet. A toilet! That's important. How many societies have fallen because of poor waste disposal? You will not be overcome by that!

You find a spare toilet seat and place it on top of a trash bucket. You place a roll of toilet paper beside it, and there you have it—your toilet. How ingenious you are. And to make sure it works, one of you uses it. Look at what you can do. Mom's got to hear about this. Won't she be so proud!

You race upstairs, shouting, "Mom, Mom, you've got to see what we did downstairs!"

She drops what she's doing as you lead her by hand.

She notices your rations and supplies, "Wow, look at this. You've thought of everything." Then she winks. "You're definitely ready for battle."

But then her eyes glance around the room. She crinkles her nose, goes *sniff, sniff,* and then says, "Do you smell that?"

You say, "Well, yes, we made a toilet!" You heave the full toilet to face level for her to see and then say, "And we've used it, too!"

Now your mother doesn't just smell its contents, she sees them too.

And you exclaim, "Aren't you so proud of us? Look what we've done!"

Sometimes good deeds aren't as good as you think. Isaiah 64:6 says, "All our righteous acts are like filthy rags." Righteous acts are the deeds you do to save yourself since committing one sin means you have committed them all.

Now let's say it is quite a few years later, and you're not a boy anymore. You're a senior in college, and you're not having fun at all. You can't remember the last time you laughed. You look in the mirror and don't recognize the person looking back at you.

You used to know what made you laugh, what made you cry, what made you angry. Now you have no clue. What is life about? It's all a haze of gray.

You're a senior in college and should be applying for jobs, but instead you drop out of school and check into a mental health facility. They say you're depressed and even more. This is a good place for you. You can't work if you're dead.

You used to roam the house with your brothers. Now you roam the halls of this house as a patient among the other patients. Manuel is tall and skinny, outgoing and friendly, the first patient who greets you. He takes you around and shows you the doctors who are nuts. Then Manuel points out the patients who are faking it. "Most of them are," he says.

Then there's Ken. Ken is hyper-suspicious of everyone, which is ironic because you're suspicious of him. He wears sunglasses and a hooded sweatshirt with the hood up, which makes him look like the Unabomber. When you approach him, he checks behind your back to make sure you're not holding a butcher knife. Not just the first time you meet him, *every* time.

And Mike. Mike's not much younger than you. He speaks softly and looks into your eyes when you talk to him. Mike seems like the kind of guy you'd like your daughter to date someday, if you have one, but you probably won't. But then Mike gets mad. He's not allowed outside for a cigarette, so he flies into a rage and turns some chairs over. The nurses place Mike in the act-out room, where Mike takes off his clothes. No, you do *not* want your improbable daughter to date Mike.

But of all the patients roaming the halls, Mark has the biggest impact on you. Admitted to the hospital by a judge's order, he was arrested for public drunkenness (not the first time). Instead of sending Mark to jail, the judge sent him here. An act of mercy, the judge called it.

"Act of mercy, whatever," Mark says to you. You're the first one he talks to.

Mark doesn't want to be here. He's doing just fine, he insists, he doesn't need counseling. So Mark mocks the work you are all doing. You bare your souls in the therapy room. You touch bone and marrow in the deepest place. You talk about matters not discussed in routine conversation. But Mark sits back and smiles. "I'm nothing like you all," he says.

As time goes on, Mark gets more agitated. He talks to you about escaping. He believes he can do it; the fence isn't that high. So sure enough, during smoke break, Mark hops the fence. His feet hit the pavement, and he runs away. The nurses herd you back inside. Later, they find Mark drunk in a bar and put him in jail.

"I'm nothing like you all," Mark had said. But you realize there's a bit of Mark in you.

Mark didn't want to look at his own raggedness. He didn't want others to help him. Mark wanted to save himself. See where it got him. You realize you'd rather flaunt your good deeds than finger your sin, but all the while, your sin is stinking up the place.

You tend to think of God as an accountant, marking down your debits and credits, adding, subtracting, and balancing the books.

God records your righteous acts—the times you help old ladies across the street, hold your tongue from slander, donate to worthwhile causes. But he also records your sinful deeds—the moments you fall short, when you abstain from doing the good you know you ought to do, when you do the bad you know is bad but do it anyway. And this accountant calculates the sum of both columns, and should the good outnumber the bad, you get your reward. You get salvation.

But what if the good deeds aren't as good as you think? What if you hobble together your magnificent works, gather the many into your shining arms, and then ask God to come and see what you have done? Surely he'll be impressed. Surely the good will outnumber the bad. Surely God will be so proud of you that he'll offer you salvation because of the sum of them all.

But God's not an accountant, and the good can never out measure the bad. Not all nice people go to heaven. If you've sinned once, you've sinned a million times. From only one sin, all judgment is against you. So what have you to offer in exchange? What have you to buy your way out of judgment? Even your righteous acts are like filthy rags. Where you see gold, God sees a bucket of poop. You have no power to save yourself.

But someone does. The prayer of confession reminds you of your Savior.

The prayer of confession is acknowledging your sin to God and then celebrating the forgiveness you have received. Such forgiveness yields salvation. Christian confession isn't complete with just the acknowledgement of sin. Anyone from the world can do that. But for confession of sin to be Christian, forgiveness must be received on account of Christ. This wells up in great celebration. In Christ, sin is absorbed. In Christ, sin is erased. In Christ, sin is no more. Therefore, every Christian confession concludes with "Hallelujah!"

King David is a good example of confession in action. You admire David. He wrote many of the psalms that you love. He was a warrior and killed Goliath. He honored his authority even when Saul tried to kill him. He pursued God relentlessly. He laid his heart out to God. It's clear why you look up to him.

But David wasn't spotless.

He saw the beautiful Bathsheba bathing on the roof. Wanting her like a ruby for his crown, David slept with her. But Bathsheba was married to Uriah, who was fighting in the war. The men were at war while David stayed at home. So David sent word for Uriah to be placed on the frontlines. Of course, he was killed. Then David took Bathsheba to be his wife. He placed the ruby in his crown, permanently.

And David thought he had gotten away with it.

But God has a way of exposing sin in order to foster repentance. He's more into your growth and goodness than you are. The prophet Nathan confronted David, and in brokenness, David confessed to God,

"Have mercy on me, O God,

because of your unfailing love.

Because of your great compassion,

blot out the stain of my sins.

Wash me clean from my guilt.

Purify me from my sin.

For I recognize my rebellion;

it haunts me day and night" (Psalm 51:1–3, NLT)

The Hebrew word for "confess" is *yadah*. According to Vine's Dictionary, the confession is not a moralistic, autobiographical list of sins but a confession of the underlying sinfulness that engulfs all mankind and separates us from Holy God. David wasn't just confessing his individual sins—coveting, lust, adultery, deceit, and murder—but his general sinfulness. He kept his penchant for rebellion before him day and night.

But David didn't end his prayer there. He prayed,

"Forgive me for shedding blood, O God who saves;

then I will joyfully sing of your forgiveness.

Unseal my lips, O LORD,

that my mouth may praise you" (Psalm 51:14–15, NLT).

David named God "The One Who Saves." He said that he would sing with joy, his mouth would praise the Lord. But in the same prayer, David admitted his darkness and praised God for his light. He did not remain in confession but moved to celebration. What was he celebrating? God himself! The reality of his forgiveness! The praiseworthy Lord! The God who makes David right! David catapulted into hallelujah!

But only because he traveled the road of confession. You see, only those who experience the night give thanks for the morning. Confession is an acknowledgment of your sin. David owned it, saying, "My sins, my guilt, my rebellion." Although it took Nathan to call him out, David took responsibility for his actions. Confession doesn't happen in a cloudy mirror; it happens when the glass is clear. Only when you look at yourself honestly and claim what is true can the power of confession begin to work. You have to own your sin.

If you don't, your sin will find you out. God has a way of exposing it. His goal is not to embarrass, hurt, or frighten you. His goal is to love you and bring you into the fullness of who he created you to be. But sin gets in the way, and God will not have it. He loves you too much. It's always better to confess rather than be found out. A soft heart is easier to work with than a hard one.

When you do sin, own it and learn from it. What got you into that situation? What need were you trying to fill? King Solomon, who was David's son, wrote in Proverbs that wisdom has a voice and the wise listen to it. Well, sin has a voice too. Listen to your sin, and let her teach you. That way you'll be ready the next time temptation comes. And it will. There are few things guaranteed in life, but one of them is temptation. Temptation isn't a sin. Jesus was tempted in every way but was without sin. But if you keep your sinfulness before you—David said his rebellion haunted him day and night—you'll be on your guard when she starts to prowl.

And she will. You'll find sin in the most innocent of places.

One day, you open the kitchen cabinet to find green marker scribbled inside. Against all odds, it turns out you have a daughter, improbable as it once seemed. Her name means resurrection because you've received new life, and every time you say her name, you breathe the reminder of your new, improbable life.

But now you've got fathering to do. You call to her, who's

four. She toddles in, short blond strands wisping. Her dimples press into her roomy cheeks.

"Yes, Daddy?"

You kneel beside her and point to the scribbles. If you blur your eyes, the lines and doodles form her name in a four-year-old kind of way. How cute, she was trying to write her name. No wait, you tell yourself. This behavior isn't appropriate. You've got to follow through, Dad. You stiffen your back and clear your throat.

"Do you know who did this?"

She squints her pretty hazel eyes, furrows her forehead in deep concentration, and then says, "Yes, the cat did it."

You grimace. "The cat did it?"

She stares back at you through marvelous marble eyes, "Yes, it was the cat."

Clever girl. Normally, saying the cat did it wouldn't have been impressive, but the cat actually has a pair of thumbs. Not human thumbs, cat thumbs. Thumbs would be useful in drawing on cabinets. Your daughter knows this. The cat was born with a genetic mutation that gave her an extra toe on each front paw. These types of cats are called Hemingways, named for the writer Ernest Hemingway, who apparently loved this kind of cat and was such a good writer because he also had thumbs. Yes, clever girl.

You imagine little kitty grasping the green marker in her paws, her thumbs steadying the marker as she sketches your daughter's name. You're about to laugh when suddenly you remember that she is lying to you. Your own flesh and blood is lying directly to your face. And she's good at it. Improbable? No, sin is found in the most innocent places.

Which is why you need a Savior. And so does your sweet daughter. And so do the rest of us. God's judgment seat is the great equalizer. You can't escape it, regardless of your charm or accolades or accomplishments. The judgment seat awaits the sinner and the saint. You'll stand before the seat—although you'll probably fall, not stand.

But Jesus did the unthinkable—he died in your place. You deserved punishment, but since you received him, you get grace, new life. And that grace opens up the kingdom of God, delivers eternal life, and welcomes you into the fellowship of the Father. God's grace is undeserved, unfathomable, unimaginable.

But wonderful as grace is, it doesn't void the judgment seat. Everyone will face it. But here's the thing—Jesus satisfies the seat. So when you appear at the judgment seat your sins will not be counted against you because, while on earth, you asked Jesus to be your Savior. Jesus will stand in your place. Above your head will be the F word, *forgiven*.

And God will say, "Welcome!" and will throw open the doors of heaven. And because you are forgiven, heaven will erupt in gladness. And so will you. Your sin did not condemn you.

You have a friend who doubts his salvation weekly, and weekly, he calls you to make sure he's still saved.

"Yes, you're still a Christian," you reassure him.

But he's not so sure. He has sinned since the last time you spoke. Has his sin canceled his salvation?

"No, it hasn't," you tell him, "Your sin is precisely the reason for your salvation."

"Yeah, you told me that last week," he says.

"Then what's the problem?"

"I keep feeling condemned."

You sigh, about to lose patience. But you remember your old days. You say, "Buddy, it seems like you're not receiving your forgiveness. God has forgiven you, but your hands are closed like you don't want to accept it. You have to walk in your forgiveness even if you don't feel like it."

But he gets off the phone quickly. He doesn't want to hear what you have to say. He'd rather live the other way. He'd rather replay the mistakes he's made like a song on repeat, heed the bully voices in his head, go by the names that are thrown at him. Who needs enemies when you can beat yourself up? You say a prayer for him.

Condemnation is cold and prickly; it doesn't feel good to the skin. It boxes your friend in and makes him walk low. You know, you've seen it. He crouches as he goes. From the tips of his toes to the crest of his head, he feels wrong through and through. Give the world time, and the world will collapse because of him, he thinks.

There's no future, only a past. There's no road out, only a road in. It swallows him up. For your friend in condemnation, the prayer of confession would be hell. Because instead of receiving his forgiveness and moving into celebration, he condemns himself for his sin. For him there is no freedom from that which binds, just stinging reminders of falling short. Start the continuous song, rally the bully voices, live by the reckless names.

But confession draws you out, the one who was hiding. You find that what you've been doing is not who you really are. And so you bring your sin before the Savior, who piles it into his arms and carries it away like firewood. Then he throws it into the fire. The ash drifts into the sky and blows in opposite directions, some to the east and some to the west. It is long gone. He doesn't want it to return.

So don't bring it back. Don't call the ash from the air and smear it on your face. Don't memorialize it in urns and place it on the mantel. Don't wear it around your neck. Don't keep your sin alive. What Jesus calls dead, leave dead.

From cradle to grave, apply the work of Jesus so you can laugh deeply as a child with no shame.

Tweets from this Chapter

» You'd rather flaunt your good deeds than finger your sin, but all the while your sin is stinking up the place. @ CSHeinz

» Not all nice people go to heaven. If you've sinned once, you've sinned a million times. @CSHeinz

» For confession of sin to be Christian, forgiveness must be received on account of Christ. This wells up in great celebration. @CSHeinz

» God has a way of exposing sin in order to foster repentance. He's more into your growth and goodness than you are. @CSHeinz

» Only when you look at yourself honestly and claim what is true can the power of confession begin to work. You have to own your sin. @CSHeinz

» Confession draws you out, the one who was hiding. You find out what you've been doing is not who you really are. @CSHeinz

» Don't keep your sin alive. What Jesus calls dead, leave dead. @CSHeinz

Discussion Questions

1. What is the definition of the prayer of confession?
2. What profession (like an accountant) describes your view of God?

3. Can you relate to Mark in the hospital? Are there any areas of your life that you have not given over to God?

4. Was there a time when someone helped you take responsibility for your actions like Nathan did for David?

5. What are the two elements of confession? Which is easier for you?

6. What does it look like to own your sin?

7. What does this mean, "But wonderful as grace is, it doesn't void the judgment seat?"

8. Are you able to receive God's full forgiveness or do you struggle with it?

9. What's the difference between conviction and condemnation?

10. Do you feel drawn to this prayer type?

10
Prayer of Thanksgiving

Thanksgiving—giving thanks in everything—prepares the
way that God might show us his fullest salvation in Christ.
—Ann Voskamp, *One Thousand Gifts*[22]

Give thanks in all circumstances, for this is
God's will for you in Christ Jesus.
—1 Thessalonians 5:18

Definition of Prayer of Thanksgiving: Offering thanks to God

Bible Character: Paul

YOU HEAR THE STORY OF a man who is accused of a crime he
didn't commit, and because he doesn't have fancy lawyers,
he goes to prison. He spends nineteen years there, and although
he didn't do what they say he did, he decides to make the most of

it. He learns to speak Spanish and to play seven instruments and earns a college degree.

He comes up for parole four times, and even though he has learned to do these civilized things and has behaved well, they're not good enough reasons for the parole board to let him go because he won't admit to doing what they think he did. They don't care that he can now speak Spanish.

But then someone with initials after his name, someone with clout and pull, goes digging around the case file and evidence box and convinces a judge to look at them. After the judge digs around them himself, he realizes the man has been telling the truth. After nineteen years, he is free to go.

So he walks out of prison. And even though his kids are all grown now, and he and his wife have missed nineteen years of living together, and he has every reason to be nasty and throw a fit, he doesn't. When the newspaper reporter asks what he thinks of all this, he says he's thankful to be home. Then he says that God is still good.

You're amazed at this man, and you know you would behave just as well in his situation.

So you're in college and have just written a paper that you think is wonderful. Your professor calls you into her office because she thinks it's wonderful too and wants to tell you to your face. Only she thinks it's *too* wonderful for your abilities and thinks you copied it from a library book or the *New Yorker*.

Now you have to deliver samples of your previous writing to prove you are capable of such work. But they have to be delivered right away, so you walk back to your room, seething red-hot and telling people how horrible your professor is, that she doesn't know anything.

You gather your best work, essays and stories, and trudge back to her den. You don't look her in the eye; you just drop the work into her bony hand and turn away to leave. She thanks you for cooperating, but you don't acknowledge her. You tell people she's worse than poison.

You get a call that she's ready to see you again, so you go back to the den. She says what you knew all along—she was wrong, and that you did write the piece. Further, she says you're a good writer, and she likes your stuff. Your heart starts to turn. But then she says you have not followed the assignment and will get a low grade. You know she's right, but you'll spread your venom anyway.

One day, you read about another man who is thrown in prison and who happens to be a writer. Something about his life intrigues you, and you know you have not behaved well. He's the apostle Paul, who was not only imprisoned, but also wrote more words in the New Testament than anyone else. And on top of that, he was also beaten, shipwrecked, almost starved to death, run out of town, and abandoned by his supporters.

If anyone had a reason to be nasty, it was Paul. You wonder how he would have acted in your position and decide probably not the way you have. You wonder what his secret was.

So you read more about him, read all the stuff he wrote, and find some patterns. You discover that despite Paul's circumstances, he kept going. He kept starting churches, preaching the gospel, and defending the truth. He kept raising people of God, appointing leaders, and demonstrating the power of God. He made it look so easy, but you know it wasn't.

You also see that Paul prayed a particular way quite often—thanksgiving. Thirteen books of the New Testament are usually attributed to Paul, and the prayer of thanksgiving is in ten of them. (The three that do not are 2 Corinthians, Galatians, and Titus). For example, Paul writes in:

» Romans: "First, I thank my God through Jesus Christ for all of you" (1:8).

» 1 Corinthians: "I always thank God for you because of his grace given you" (1:4).

» Ephesians: "I have not stopped giving thanks for you" (1:16).

Then he goes on in:

» Philippians: "I thank my God every time I remember you" (1:3).

» Colossians: "We always thank God, the Father of our Lord Jesus Christ, when we pray for you" (1:3).

» 1 Thessalonians: "We always thank God for all of you" (1:2).

» 2 Thessalonians: "We ought to always thank God for you" (1:3).

And some more in:

» 1 Timothy: "I thank Christ Jesus our Lord, who has given me strength" (1:12).

» 2 Timothy: "I thank God, whom I serve, with a clear conscience, as night and day I constantly remember you in my prayers" (1:3).

» Philemon 4: "I always thank my God as I remember you in my prayers."

Wow, Paul was such a thankful guy. He prayed the prayer of thanksgiving so often, which is simply offering thanks to God. Not only did Paul practice the prayer of thanksgiving in his personal faith, he encouraged others to do the same. Paul was a church planter and a spiritual father, and he asked his spiritual children to imitate his way of life. He said to give thanks in all circumstances because it is God's will for them in Christ Jesus (1 Thessalonians 5:18).

But why is it God's will for them to be thankful? And why was Paul so dedicated to the prayer of thanksgiving? What was the payoff?

Let's say you're waiting for your plane to Tokyo on your mission trip to Myanmar (formerly Burma). You're the leader of the group. The announcer says the plane will arrive two hours late, but this is a problem because you only have an hour layover in Tokyo to catch your flight to Bangkok.

You discuss your issue with the lady at the desk. She has already placed your group on another flight to Bangkok. The problem is, you arrive into Bangkok ten hours later than your original ticket, and so you'll miss your flight to Myanmar. And the Myanmar flight is on another ticket.

You're the team leader. Worry sets in. What will you do?

You e-mail your prayer team. It will take an act of God for the flights to work out. As you hit Send, an e-mail comes in. It's from a book publisher. For the last year, you've sent out proposals for a book on prayer to twenty-four publishers. Until now, you've received twenty-three rejections.

But you feel really good about this one. All that's left is a final meeting and a final decision, and here it is. You open the e-mail, needing good news. But it's rejection twenty-four.

You sink into your seat; an impossible circumstance, a discouraging situation. You feel weighed down by these burdens. There's no way this plane will take off with your extra baggage. Then you sense a still, small voice getting your attention. It says to press into the Prince of Peace. You have a decision to make. Will you press into Jesus or be consumed by your circumstances?

You've been in this situation before, not on a plane with eager missionaries, but in the plain of choice. You have sat on the edge of decision. One way is to plunge fully ahead into Jesus, running to him because he's the only choice. Or you can go the other way, trying to work it out on your own. Maybe you can muster up the magic to save the day. It's your college course all over again, your professor putting you to the test. God putting you to the test. God does promise to test your heart.

You remember a verse your mama taught you. She'd say do not worry about anything, but in everything, with thanksgiving, present your requests to God—a paraphrase of Philippians 4:6. Then she would tell you the grand result of such activity: The peace of God, which extends above and beyond all understanding, will guard your heart and mind in Christ Jesus—verse seven.

She always said this with great confidence, like she knew what would happen if you traded in your worry for surrender. Not a passive surrender like you're throwing up your arms ambivalently, but rather an active surrender like you know what you're doing and all the while full of thanksgiving. It seemed like giving thanks was a good choice for her. Life was not all roses and doubloons for her. She struggled.

But it's how she handled her struggles that impressed you. She had ample right to complain, seek pity, and throw her arm across her forehead and sigh like a fainting debutante. But she didn't. She gave thanks in everything instead. You wonder, is there some of her in you? You certainly hope so. Your mama had the most amazing faith. And her smile could light up the night.

Thanksgiving makes peace, she would say, and if you don't live for Jesus, what's the point of his dying? Suddenly, Mama is the smartest one in the room. You didn't take seriously her words before, but now their relevance and wisdom and strength are crashing down on you. You want Jesus to guard your heart and mind. He died to do that, so why not let him?

Oh, you haven't lived in peace. You've lived by other masters. You've let your circumstances and relationships and spiritual warfare consume you. You've bound yourself to your afflictions and burdened yourself with your troubles. It was always someone else's fault—bad moon rising, bad luck, bad cards dealt to you. You haven't lived a life that echoed your salvation.

As a Christian, peace is your inheritance. An inheritance isn't given unless someone dies. Jesus died for your peace, so live it. But your life doesn't echo this inheritance. "If you're not gonna live for Jesus, what's the point of his dying?" Mama would say. What would she say now?

She'd say to run after it and never let it go. She'd say peace is the mark of the Christian. It's the way of the cross. The point of the cross was to bring peace between God and creation. Where once there was enmity and divide, the cross brought peace. And this Savior has made himself your peace, so don't waste it. Pursue peace like it's your calling. Live in such a way that your life echoes your salvation. You can hear Mama speaking now. So you press into Jesus with thanksgiving.

You thank Jesus for giving you peace as an inheritance. You thank him for directing your steps. He's Lord over your life—this distressing plane ride and frustrating process with the book. You thank him for the opportunity to travel and to write, even if those publishers don't know a good thing when they see it. You thank him for Mama.

And as you do, you experience the benefits of your salvation. Peace descends upon you and warms your heart. Your mind feels secure, and you're convinced that things will work out. You're not worried anymore because the Prince of Peace is in control. You don't need these publishers or an on-time arrival into Myanmar. You can trust him.

Thanksgiving assures you that Jesus is enough. It has changed your perspective.

Suddenly, everywhere you look you see little gifts from God. You breathe in and thank God for breath because somewhere someone's breath has left her. You stretch out your legs and thank God you can because somewhere someone's legs have failed him. You look out the window and thank God for the sky because somewhere someone's sight has failed her. You wonder how many gifts you've missed because you didn't realize they were gifts.

You think of Mama again. Mama said that thanksgiving was a sacrifice that disciplined the flesh. Those were meaty words from Mama, but they sound true. So you pull out your Bible to see what she meant. You open the concordance in the back and find verses for "thanks."

> » You turn to Psalm 56:1, "I am under vows to you, O God; I will present thank offerings to you."
> » Then Psalm 107:22, "Let them sacrifice thank offerings and tell of his works with songs of joy."
> » And finally Psalm 116:17, "I will sacrifice a thank offering to you and call on the name of the LORD."

You never thought of thanksgiving as a sacrifice before. It's always been a feeling. But biblical thanksgiving is more of a choice than a feeling. A choice you haven't made.

When you didn't feel like being thankful, you weren't. You were thankful when you wanted to be, when you got your way, when a reward was obvious. But these verses blow these childish ideas out of the sky. Here the thank offering is something that is vowed, a deliberate decision regardless of your mood. Yes, thanksgiving is a choice. Go, Mama!

You read on to discover that the thank offering was a regular means of sacrifice in the Bible. When King David prepared for the temple to be built, he set aside the Levites as priests. One of their duties was to thank God every morning and evening because gratitude must flow in the house of God (1 Chronicles 23:30).

When Hezekiah cleansed and restored the temple, he ordered people to bring sacrifices and thank offerings. Now that the temple was in order, Hezekiah reinstated the practice that David instituted—thanksgiving (2 Chronicles 29:31).

When the wall of Jerusalem was repaired, Nehemiah assigned two choirs to give thanks. He placed one choir at the Gate of the Guard and the other at the Dung Gate. The Dung Gate was where waste was gathered and removed from the city. It wasn't a pleasant place. If you can give thanks at the Dung Gate, you can give thanks anywhere (Nehemiah 12:31).

Before Jesus performed one of the greatest miracles ever, multiplying five loaves and two fishes into a feast for over five thousand people, he gave thanks to God (Matthew 14:19). At the Last Supper with his disciples on the eve of his crucifixion, Jesus gave thanks again (Matthew 26:26–27).

And you've already read about Paul. Not only was the prayer of thanksgiving in ten of his thirteen books, but he taught his churches to be thankful too. Wow, the prayer of thanksgiving is rampant throughout the Bible, active in the lives of Old and New Testament believers, and encouraged as a way of life.

You decide to try it some more. But rather than pick an easy thanksgiving, you'll put yourself to the test. The value you place on thanksgiving, and really anything God says, is revealed in the tough times. The easy times don't reveal very much. It's the hard times that show what's really going on. If you really believe in giving thanks at all times, give thanks where it's hardest—at the Dung Gate.

What's your Dung Gate? At the Dung Gate, you give thanks in all circumstances, which is different from giving thanks for all circumstances. The apostle Paul said to give thanks *in* all things. He didn't say to give thanks *for* all things. God is not asking you to give thanks for the storm that destroyed your home, but he is asking you to give thanks in it. There are blessings even in that, and thanksgiving uncovers them.

So what's your Dung Gate? It's the situation with your son.

No, you can't go there. You can't possibly. What good is that? But you know you must.

Paul would, Mama would, and you should. Hidden gifts, triumphant peace, new perspective might all be waiting for you at the Dung Gate.

The Dung Gate is where you don't want to go but is where you experience the blessings of deliberate thanksgiving. Not many people choose to go there, but your path now leads there. Maybe this delayed plane ride is a setup to get you to stop at the Dung Gate. Now you must go.

You continue walking toward it.

"Heavenly Father, I thank you for my son."

You pause, catching your breath.

"He wasn't born like the rest, wasn't born whole. It hasn't been easy."

Already trickles of tears are running down your face. You think of fleeing but decide to stay.

"I thank you for the plan you have for our son. It's different than the plan I would have chosen."

You realize that when your son was born, you thought of it as an ending rather than a beginning.

"Father, thank you for the glorious beginning of his new life. From the start, I thought of all the things he wouldn't be able to do. But that was wrong. Every new creation is good."

You remember your envious glances at other kids and their parents. You wanted to be like them, have a normal life.

"I thank you for our way of life. It's not the same as others because it's our life, and you have given it to us."

Then you think of the times of prayer and soul-searching discussions that you and your wife have shared. You have come to love her so deeply because of your son.

"Father, thank you for how my wife and I have grown in love. Our son has enabled us to go deeper than I ever thought possible."

And what of yourself? This has taken a toll on you. You've felt blemished as a man. Why couldn't you produce a normal child? You've felt powerless. Why can't you fix him? You've felt less than a man, a big phony. You shift in your seat; you want to run from the Dung Gate. But you don't.

"Father, I thank you for the man you have made me, but mostly for the man I'm becoming. I thank you for the experiences that have built my character and have made me who I am. I thank you for showing me what really makes a man."

The pilot's voice comes over the speaker, stirring you from your place of thought and prayer. The plane will be landing soon, and you wonder what will happen with your trip. It doesn't matter.

You've already come a long distance. You're becoming the person you want to be.

Tweets from this Chapter

» Not only did the Apostle Paul practice thanksgiving prayer in his personal faith, he encouraged others to do the same. @CSHeinz

» As a Christian, peace is your inheritance. An inheritance isn't given unless someone dies. Jesus died for your peace, so live it. @CSHeinz

» Pursue peace like it's your calling. Live in such a way that your life echoes your salvation. @CSHeinz

» Thanksgiving assures you that Jesus is enough. @CSHeinz

» Biblical thanksgiving is more of a choice than a feeling. @CSHeinz

» The value you place on thanksgiving, and really anything God says, is revealed in the tough times. @CSHeinz

» If you really believe in giving thanks at all times, then give thanks where it's hardest—at the Dung Gate. What's your Dung Gate? @CSHeinz

Discussion Questions

1. What is the definition of the prayer of thanksgiving?
2. What keeps you from offering thanksgiving more often?
3. When did you pray the prayer of thanksgiving? What was the result?
4. For you, is thanksgiving more of a discipline or a joy?
5. According to the book of Philippians, what is the by-product of thanksgiving?
6. Why do you think Paul prayed thanksgiving so often?
7. In what areas of your life is thanksgiving easy?
8. Does your life have any dung gates? In what areas is thanksgiving difficult?
9. What would a prayer of thanksgiving for a difficult area sound like?
10. Do you feel drawn to this prayer type?

11
Praying in Tongues

Your spirit longs to speak to God, so speak to him! You
don't always have to know what you're praying about. Just
pray! Speak to God and then speak to God some more.
—Mary Alice Isleib, *Effective Fervent Prayer*[23]

If I pray in a tongue, my spirit prays.
—1 Corinthians 14:14

Definition of Praying in Tongues: Praying in a personal spiritual
language that edifies you and your relationship with God

Bible Character: The apostle Paul

YOU'VE HEARD IT SAID THAT if you keep doing the same things,
you will get the same results. That's fine if you want the same
results. But you don't. Your faith is languishing.

You've just come off a hard year—a broken relationship that

you messed up followed by excruciating soul-searching followed by depression drowned in alcohol followed by therapy in a mental health program. They locked the doors after you walked through. The day you checked in was October 31.

The therapy was good. You're not depressed anymore. You got a lot of answers. And you're not binge drinking anymore. But despite this, you're still not happy. You decide to do something desperate—you sign up for a Christian conference that is beyond your comfort zone. You've only heard about what the conference is promoting, you've never seen it.

You walk into the first session and already you're uncomfortable. There's lightning in the air. Passionate worship fills the space. Hands are raised, waving, swirling in motion. People are on their feet. Tears run from some of their eyes. A few of them kneel at the front. They lie on the ground. This is not what you're used to.

You find a seat and try to sing the words, "Lord, I give you my heart," but your heart's not on the Lord, it's on the people around you. What's going on? Why are they so hyped? A man in front of you turns around and says he'd like to tell you something.

"Is that okay?" he asks.

How do you know if it's okay if you don't know what he's about to tell you?

But you say yes because you're curious. Plus these people seem pretty harmless. This is starting to grow on you. There's freedom and liberty here. The people don't seem to care at all if makeup is running down their faces or if they're getting dirty from lying on the ground. There could be worse things. They only seem to care about worshipping God.

That has not been the case for you.

So after you say yes, the man says, "Son, the Lord has a word for you."

You think, *He does? Then why doesn't he tell me himself?* You're not used to God speaking to other people about you. But if God wants to say something to you, you want to hear it. You tell him to go ahead.

The man proceeds to spill the secrets of your heart onto the floor. He whispers sacred things that you have only told God. They're fragile. They're not easy. They're special to you. And now God is saying them back to you through this messenger. Through your hard year, you thought you were alone. But now you see that God was there.

Your heart is pounding now, pounding with hot and heavy heat. You feel the words of your Father penetrate you. Can words be alive? They're echoing throughout your soul. *Your Father was there, your Father was there.* And more, your Father is here. In this auditorium, God has called you his own.

When you open your eyes, you realize the man has stopped talking and has returned to worshipping. Things don't seem so strange anymore. The worship ends, and then a sermon is given. After that, the ministry team invites people on stage to receive prayer.

When they say "receive prayer," they mean receive the baptism of the Holy Spirit.

You're open to new things, but not that open. You've seen the television shows—a minister places his hand on a person's forehead, person shakes, person falls down. It's so dramatic, and isn't it convenient that the cameraman manages to catch it on film? You're convinced the minister pushed the person over. Or the person fell on purpose. It's good for ratings.

So no, thank you. You will not go onstage and be prayed for. You'll watch the entertainment from a distance and blow the whistle on them.

One by one people go up. Most of them fall down. But it's different from what you expected. There's no pushing, no cameramen, no one appears to be falling on purpose. The atmosphere feels gentle and sweet.

Maybe you'll give it a try. I mean, you've come all this way. And you do need a change. And God did meet you in your conference seat. Will he meet you on the stage too?

You step into the line that leads to the stage. Slowly, you inch your way to the front until you are there. All along you've watched the minister and nothing seems shady. Different, yes. Suspicious, no. Let's see how it goes for you.

You decide not to go down easily. You'll plant your legs, tense your body, and will not go down without a fight. You'll tighten your stomach like a muscle man about to receive a cannonball into it. You will not be pushed over. When it's your turn, you steady yourself, half of you wanting to be pushed and expose this whole sham and the other half wanting it to be real and embrace it.

The minister says, "You'll be a light to your generation," and softly blows on your face. You hit the floor. So much for steady! Later, you'll remember how heavy the invisible weight pressing on your shoulders was and how weak your knees suddenly became. You'll remember how your heart felt like fire, and your body was no match for such heat. You'll remember how God never felt so close, and that the minister never even touched you.

You lie there awhile, bathing in beauty, basking in light. You've never felt at once so little and at the same time so loved. The presence of God is surrounding you. You feel like God's son.

After you compose yourself, you get up and take the bus to the hotel. Your roommate is waiting for you. You don't really know him. He was your randomly assigned roommate. But maybe with God nothing is random, so you'll soon find out.

"How was your evening?" he asks.

"Well if you really want to know, you'd better get comfortable," you say.

You realize it's going to be a long night. You explain everything, and as you do, he laughs gleefully. He can relate. After you're through, you say, "It was amazing. Now where is it in the Bible?"

He laughs again. "I hoped you would ask. Now *you* had better get comfortable."

He then takes you on a tour of the Bible, showing you emphatic worship, passionate prayer, prophetic words, and finally baptism of the Holy Spirit. He says Elizabeth, the mother of John the Baptist, was filled with the Holy Spirit when she greeted Mary, who was pregnant with Jesus (Luke 1:41). He also says that John the Baptist said that Jesus would baptize with the Holy Spirit and with fire (Luke 3:16).

Then he smiles and says, "There's one more thing I think God wants to do."

"What's that?" You can't think of anything more God could possibly do.

"One of the last things Jesus said to his disciples was that believers will pray in new tongues. That's in Mark 16:17. I think God wants to give you a prayer language."

"A prayer language?"

"Yes, let me explain."

So you talk longer about the Bible and finally you say, "I'd like that," so he prays for you and what starts as foolish-sounding grunts becomes a shooting stream of fire.

It's like someone turned the engine on or added gasoline and the spring that has been gaining steam has been suddenly untapped. You begin to pray from the deep well of your spirit, and the more you do, the more energized you feel.

These are not English or even human words. They are unrecognizable. But they're from your spirit.

He turns out the light, "I'm going to bed. You should stay up and do this more. You can pray in tongues whenever you want to."

So you stay up longer and pray with your spirit even though it's already morning. And when you return home, you know you're different. Others see it too.

Praying in tongues is praying in a personal spiritual language that edifies you and your relationship with God.

At the conference you had the crash course. Now you want to investigate further. Not because you doubt your new prayer language, but so you can understand it better. Your friends are asking questions. They want to know why you're different, lighter, joyful, stronger. But you don't know what to tell them. You need more time.

As you study, you learn some interesting things. There are three kinds of tongues in the Bible:

>   Speaking in a language you have not learned

>   Delivering a message from God in tongues

>   Praying to God in your own spiritual language

The first is speaking in a language you have not learned. In Acts 2, a group of Jesus followers were filled with the Holy Spirit and began to speak in other tongues. Visitors from other nations heard them and were amazed because they heard their native languages that were foreign to the believers.

The scene was so crazy that onlookers thought they were drunk. But Peter stood up and addressed the crowd. Quoting from the book of Joel, he said, "In the last days, 'God says, I will pour out my Spirit on all people … I will show wonders in the heaven above and signs on the earth below." God poured out his Spirit on them. Just like he said he would.

In the period of time after Jesus resurrected and before he ascended to heaven, he spent forty days with the disciples. One of the instructions he gave them was, "Do not leave Jerusalem, but wait for the gift my Father promised, which you have heard me speak about. For John baptized with water, but in a few days you will be baptized with the Holy Spirit" (Acts 1:4–5). Jesus told them they would receive the Spirit if they waited in Jerusalem.

What were they doing when the Spirit came? They were waiting for their gift. And now that the gift had come, what did it bring? Speaking in a language they had not learned. Tongues of fire rested on each of them, enabling them to speak a different language. It was a sign of God's kingdom, precisely the purpose of the Spirit's outpouring in Joel.

But this isn't a prayer language.

A second kind of tongues is delivering a message from God in tongues. For this to be helpful, it must be interpreted. The ability to interpret a message given in tongues is a unique spiritual gift. This kind of tongue functions like a prophetic word. Its purpose is to communicate a message from God and just happens to be in tongues.

But without interpretation, the message can't be understood, which is why the apostle Paul instructed, "If anyone speaks in a tongue, two—or at the most three—should speak, one at a time, and someone must interpret. If there is no interpretation, the speaker should keep quiet in the church and speak to himself and God" (1 Corinthians 14:27–28).

The purpose of this kind of tongue is for God to communicate a message. But instead of using one messenger, he uses two—one for hearing and speaking the message and the other for interpreting and speaking the message. God's desire is to build his body. Again, the tongue functions as a sign of God's kingdom, but not only that, the built-up body does as well. The unified body signifies God's work among its members. With this kind of tongue, God gets two signs for the price of one.

But this isn't a prayer language either.

The third kind of tongue is the prayer language. The apostle
Paul is a biblical character who prayed in tongues. He wrote, "If I
pray in a tongue, my spirit prays" (1 Corinthians 14:14) and "I thank
God that I speak in tongues more than all of you" (1 Corinthians
14:18). Paul was glad for the gift of tongues in his life.

You know Paul the missionary and Paul the apostle, but
do you know Paul the tongues-speaker? Paul is known for
planting churches, raising leaders, and evangelizing the Greeks.
He's known for apologetics, persecution, and theology. Paul was
sophisticated and schooled. But praying in tongues seems so,
well... unsophisticated. It sounds unsophisticated when you hear it
and even more when you try it. Why would Paul pray in tongues?
Why would this spiritual icon grunt out prayers to God?

Sometimes human language isn't adequate to communicate
with God. Praying in tongues is like spiritual poetry. Regular
words fail when trying to express love, ecstasy, another emotion,
or a desire that is presently overwhelming you. The idea is so
large it currently transcends your ability to express it. How shall
you speak to your lover when no words will do? You write
poetry.

Praying in tongues helps you pray greater than human words
allow. Why should human words be all you need? Why should
human words be all you have? Your relationship with God is the
epic romance. Forget Romeo and Juliet, Jack and Rose, Rhett
and Scarlett. God is in love with you. So much that he sent his
only son to die for you—even when the son asked to get out of
it. And he wants you to love him back. So sometimes only poetry
will do.

Your essence is not flesh; it's spirit. And God is not flesh;
he's spirit. Praying in tongues is the language of the spirit. Paul
wrote, "So what shall I do? I will pray with my spirit, but I will
also pray with my mind" (1 Corinthians 14:15). When you pray

in tongues, you pray from your spirit to God's Spirit. And God's Spirit understands what your spirit is praying, even if you don't.

You're a citizen of heaven, a child of God, a spiritual being. You were made by God for God. Your relationship with God is primary, all else is secondary. There is no more important, proper, or dignified pursuit than to grow in your walk with God. "But you, dear friends, build yourselves up in your most holy faith and pray in the Holy Spirit," says Jude 1:20.

Does that mean you need to pray in tongues to walk with God? No. There are more people in the Bible for whom tongues is never mentioned than for whom it is. There are scores of spiritually mature people who love God with their whole heart and have never prayed in tongues. There are probably more people you look up to who don't pray in tongues. Growth in God is not dependent on praying in tongues. Neither is salvation—that comes only through Christ.

Praying in tongues does not make someone more saved. If you're alive, you're alive. If you're dead, you're dead. And if you're saved, you're saved. When you stand before God after passing from this earth, he does not say, "She prayed in tongues, so I'm going to let her in." No, he says, "I see my Son instead of her sin. Come on in."

Tongues cannot add or detract from the fact of your salvation, but they can improve the experience of your salvation. Tongues are given by God to certain people in certain times. They're a spiritual gift that is given through the wisdom of God. He gives it to some people who never ask for it.

There was a young woman, a waitress from Outback, whose table customers befriend her. She seems downcast, and they reach out to her. They invite her over and ultimately she decides to follow Jesus. They invite other believers over, and they baptize her in their bathtub. Then she comes downstairs for them to bless her.

The group of believers lay hands on her and begin to thank God for her salvation. They ask God's Spirit to fill her. As soon as they do, she begins praying in tongues. No one has spoken to her about this, no one has taught her. The deep groans and flicks of joy spring from her spirit like grand affirmations of a heavenly home. Human words won't do when her spirit is soaring.

In Acts 2:4, as soon as the believers were filled with the Holy Spirit, they began to speak in tongues. In Acts 19:6, Paul baptized believers in the name of Jesus, and when he laid hands on them, they began speaking in tongues. None of these believers had been taught about tongues nor had they asked to receive the gift of tongues. God decided to pour it out when he poured out the Holy Spirit.

But tongues do not always accompany the baptism of the Holy Spirit. No one prays in tongues without being baptized in the Spirit, but not everyone who has been baptized in the Spirit prays in tongues. In Acts 4:31, the believers were praying together in one place, and the place was shaken, and they were all filled with the Holy Spirit. But the Bible doesn't say they spoke in tongues.

In Acts 9:17, Ananias was praying for God to restore the eyesight of Saul (who would become Paul), and he prayed for Saul to be filled with the Holy Spirit, but there is no mention of tongues at the time. Likewise, when Elizabeth, mother of John the Baptist, was filled with the Holy Spirit, tongues did not follow.

On the other hand, sometimes God withholds tongues from people who ask for it. Even to people who've been asking for years. To those who don't understand why he won't give them this gift. They see how someone received tongues so effortlessly and wonder why God doesn't do the same for them. They search their heart for hidden sin, pump up the level of their praise, and keep asking. But God doesn't answer.

Maybe that's the point. Sometimes God withholds an answer to prayer in order to produce deeper holiness, discipleship, praise, or even desperation. Maybe he knows you're better off that way first. And when the process has done its work, he'll pour it out. Only he sees what's around the corner.

As you type out your thoughts on tongues, you receive an e-mail from someone you met at the conference. She's a grandmotherly sort who came over to you during one of the breaks. She saw your hesitation on the first night but noticed a complete turnaround the next day and wanted to know what happened. You explained it all, cutting into the next session.

Now she writes, "Dearie, keep pressing into God. What he began in you, follow until completion. And don't stop praying with your spirit. I didn't tell you this—my mom passed away when I was twelve years old. The night she passed away, she was speaking in tongues up until her last breath. I was standing at the end of her bed and that made a big impact on my life. So don't back down when God is up to something."

What a way to go out—fellowshipping in this life right into the next, spirit to Spirit, until you're face-to-face with God.

You think back to that conference night when you walked in a doubter and walked out undignified. That night was October 31. And you realize it was exactly one year to the day that you checked into the hospital because you needed something more. God has been working all along.

Tweets from this Chapter

> » Sometimes human language isn't adequate to communicate with God. Praying in tongues is like spiritual poetry. @ CSHeinz

» Praying in tongues helps you pray what is greater than human words allow. Your relationship with God is the epic romance after all. @CSHeinz

» Your essence is not flesh, it's spirit. And God is not flesh, he's spirit. Praying in tongues is the language of the spirit. @CSHeinz

» The gift of tongues cannot add or detract from the fact of your salvation, but it can improve the experience of your salvation. @CSHeinz

» We know Paul the Missionary and Paul the Apostle, but do we know Paul the Tongues-Speaker? He spoke in tongues more than anyone. @CSHeinz

» Sometimes God withholds an answer to prayer in order to produce in us deeper holiness, discipleship, praise, or even desperation. @CSHeinz

Discussion Questions

1. What is the definition of praying in tongues?
2. Before you read this chapter, what did you think and how did you feel about tongues?
3. What are the three types of tongues in the Bible?
4. What can get in the way of someone praying in tongues?
5. Do you think praying in tongues was important to Paul? What role did tongues play in his life and ministry?
6. Do you pray in tongues? If so, what was your experience in learning how to pray in the Spirit?
7. Praying in tongues is probably the most controversial of the prayer types. Why is this?

8. If we don't have to pray in tongues to be saved, why pray in tongues at all?

9. Do you think God gives the gift of tongues to everyone who asks? Why or why not?

10. Do you feel drawn to this prayer type?

12

Prayer of Agreement

Agreement begins with a God focus and a heart
that is close to him. When your heart is knit to the
LORD, he then will knit you together to accomplish
more than you could ever accomplish alone.
—Beth Alves, *Becoming a Prayer Warrior*[24]

I tell you that if you agree about anything you ask for, it will
be done for you by my Father in heaven. For where two or
three come together in my name, there am I with them.
—Matthew 18:19–20

Definition of Prayer of Agreement: Multiple believers agreeing
on Earth with what heaven is saying

Bible Character: The Church in Acts

*R*ING, RING. THE CALLER ID says it's your friend. You don't
talk very often, but when you do, it's usually important,
so you answer the call.

"What's up, buddy?" you ask.

His voice is hushed. "Hey, I don't have long, but will you pray for me? You're the first person I thought of."

"Sure, what's going on?"

He tells you his job has taken him to a risky place, a place full of sinners and sin, and while he won't be participating in the activities, it's not a place he'd like to be. His boss chose him to go because your friend is a Christian. He didn't send your friend to minister but because the boss is messing with him. He wants to make your friend feel uncomfortable. Done.

Your friend is calling from the bathroom. Of course you'll pray.

"Can we pray now?" you ask.

"Yes, you pray, and I'll agree with you."

So you begin, "Lord, you didn't promise to keep us from danger, but I pray you keep my brother from harm. You say where sin abounds, grace abounds all the more. This is the perfect opportunity for your grace."

He says, "Yes, Lord."

You go on, "God, you say to bring light into the darkness, that darkness can't put out the light, but light can put out the darkness."

"Amen, Lord."

"And God, I pray my brother would be a blessing. You say to bless those who curse you. You say to be a blessing because blessing changes the spiritual climate. We want the spiritual climate to change."

"Yes we do, Lord."

You go on, and when you finish, you both say, "Amen."

He thanks you and hangs up the phone.

According to Vine's Dictionary, when God said amen in the Bible, it meant "It is and shall be," and when people said amen, it meant "so let it be." Amen said by God is a word of establishment, while amen said by man is a word of agreement. The prayer of amen is shorthand for the prayer of agreement.

Although other prayer types were operating on the phone call—praying the Bible and petition prayer—the prayer of agreement was the predominant prayer type. Agreement prayer always partners with another prayer type. But not only that, it strengthens it. Agreement prayer buffs up other ways of praying.

When you prayed the Bible ("where sin abounds, grace abounds more"), you prayed what God was saying. This is God's amen because according to Isaiah 55:11, God's Word always accomplishes what it was sent for. God's Word is always, "it is and shall be." It is always established according to Isaiah.

But when your friend prayed with you, "Yes, Lord. Amen," this was the prayer of agreement. This was your amen. Your prayer aligned with the established Word. The prayer of agreement is multiple believers agreeing on Earth with what heaven is saying. The results of agreement prayer are incredibly powerful.

In the book of Acts, people were healed of impossible infirmities, thousands came into the kingdom in a day, people were raised from the dead, and the Holy Spirit poured out on the masses. And although Jesus wasn't on earth—he was in heaven—all of these amazing things were performed by the believers. How did these miracles happen?

The book of Acts is the book of agreement prayer. All the time, the believers were praying together. Acts 1:14 says they all joined together constantly in prayer. Acts 2:1 says when Pentecost came, 120 of them were together in one place. Acts 2:42 says they devoted themselves to daily prayer together. In Acts 4:24, the believers raised their voices together in prayer, and the place where they were meeting was shaken.

The believers were of one heart and mind in Acts 4:32.

When Peter was arrested, the believers were earnestly praying for him until an angel let him out in Acts 12:5. And in Acts 13:3, a group of leaders prayed together to release the apostle Paul on his first missionary journey. The Acts church operated on agreement prayer.

In order to achieve such tremendous growth and perform such amazing miracles, the Acts church knew how to align with heaven. They brought heaven to earth. There are three levels of alignment in agreement prayer: personally aligning with God, walking in peace with each other, and corporately aligning with heaven.

The first level is personally aligning yourself with God. Ephesians 2:6 says that God raised you up with Christ and seated you with him in the heavenly places. Philippians 3:20 says you're a citizen of heaven. As a Christian, you're seated in heaven already. You don't have to die to get to heaven; you're already there. For Christians, the issue is not doing more to get to heaven but rather becoming more aware of the heavenly position you have already. You are seated with Jesus now!

This means great favor with God because you're seated with Christ. But it also brings favor with God when you align your heart with God's purposes. When Jesus was in the temple at twelve years old, he stayed back when Mary and Joseph went ahead because he wanted to be about his Father's business. The same happens in heaven. When you're seated in heaven, you go about your Father's business.

You find out what God is establishing, and then you agree with it. You see where God is at work, and you join him. This is the key to bringing heaven down to Earth. Since you're seated in heavenly places, you're actually praying from heaven, though physically you're praying on earth. Bringing heaven down to earth is much easier when you're praying from heaven.

But just because you're a Christian doesn't mean you're about your Father's business. In Matthew 7:21, Jesus said not everyone who calls him Lord will enter heaven when they die, but only those who do the will of God. They will remind God of all the things they did on earth—prophesy, drive out demons, perform many miracles—but Jesus will say, "I never knew you. Away from me, you evildoers!"

Imagine that! Jesus will shoo away those who did not one miracle but many miracles because they were not doing the will of God.

God has a track record on this. In Acts 5, landowners Ananias and Sapphira kept money for themselves after they said they gave it all away. They were part of the communal church that shared everything. But they lied and stole, so Ananias and Sapphira dropped dead.

In Genesis 11, the people of Babel decided to make a great name for themselves by building a tower to the heavens. But God alone had the great name. So God confused their speech and scattered them across the earth. And in Genesis 19, Lot's wife looked back from where she had come rather than where God was taking her, and she turned into a pillar of salt. The people of God must be about the Father's business.

The key passage for the prayer of agreement is Matthew 18:19–20. Unfortunately, these verses are often misunderstood, so they lose their power in practical application and less people engage in agreement prayer. Jesus said, "I tell you that if you agree about anything you ask for, it will be done for you by my Father in heaven. For where two or three come together in my name, there am I with them."

These verses are often understood to be about presence, but they're actually about agreement.

Usually the prayer goes something like this, "Jesus, we're getting ready to eat this church potluck meal, and since there are more than two of us gathered, we know you're with us." But what if a person was eating alone? Does the lone person eating a sandwich in her break room not have Jesus with her?

Didn't Jesus promise to be with us even until the end of the age? Yes he did. The presence of Jesus is already promised to those who believe. Plus, the lone believer is already seated with Jesus in heaven. So Jesus can't be talking about presence. Instead, he's talking about agreement. Those who come together in his name are aligned with heaven.

The second level of alignment is walking in peace with each other. Matthew 18 says, "Where two or three come together in my name ..." It's not enough to have multiple people in the same room. If it was, any office pool that wanted to win the lottery could just ask God and he would do it. Or any sports team that wanted to win would ask God and they would get victory. Just having two or more people present does not do it. This verse is not about presence, it's about agreement.

When believers come together in Jesus' name, they gather in obedience to Jesus. Jesus said that if you come to pray and you realize your brother has something against you, or you have something against your brother, leave prayer and be reconciled to your brother. Then come back to prayer. He also said if you don't forgive others, God won't forgive you. You cannot walk together in peace if you have open accounts with each other. The prayer of agreement requires you to walk in harmony with each other.

This isn't easy. At a recent church service, one man starts clapping so loud it gives you a headache. The on-beat, mostly offbeat pounding of his palms is so distracting it sends your mood and manners into a tailspin. You try to recover your joy and thankfulness for the goodness of God, but all you can think of is why in the world did God give this guy hands.

Babies cry and screech during the service. The lady in your

row gets up three times to go to the bathroom. The bad breath from the guy behind you rots the air like garbage fumes. The people you met three weeks ago have forgotten your name. And the woman with the beehive hairdo can't stop exclaiming, "Hallelujah!" It's such a beautiful day, "Hallelujah!" God is so good, "Hallelujah!" I just got diagnosed with cancer and my dog died this morning, "Hallelujah!"

Who are these people anyway? And who invited them? You can't stand any of them; they're so annoying. But it gets worse. God says they're family because you have the same Father. He says bad breath man is your brother and hallelujah, beehive lady is your sister. The people who can't remember your name are family, and so is Mrs. Tiny Bladder. Even Happy Clapper is family. What is God thinking?

At the end of his time on earth, Jesus prayed that all believers would be one so the world would know the gospel was true (John 17:20–21). Not only are you all family, your unity preaches the gospel better than any words can. Agreement between believers is a sign of the kingdom. If you can get along, it's proof that God can change a heart. There are lots of differences, and these differences often divide believers.

> » Color or race: You have light skin, but they have dark skin.
>
> » Church denomination: You're Baptist, but they're Catholic.
>
> » Religious practice: You worship with modern music, but they use classical music.
>
> » Age: You're young, but he's in his twenties.
>
> » Educational background: You have a PhD, but he only has a high school diploma.
>
> » Personalities: You're extroverted, but they're introverted.

» Job: You have a desk job, but he's unemployed.

» Married or single: You're married, but they're single.

» Kids or no kids: You don't want kids, but they have four screaming brats.

» Spiritual gifts: You're good at evangelism, but they're not.

» Handicapped: You can use your legs, but she's in a wheelchair.

» Sanctuary: You call it a sanctuary, but they call it a worship room.

» Smartphones: You read the Bible in a book, but she reads it on her smartphone.

» Communion: You drink grape juice, but they drink wine.

» Baptism: You dunk, but they drizzle.

» Prayer Types: You enjoy listening prayer, but they wage warfare prayer.

But what you have in common with other believers is stronger than your differences. Agreement is a special force of the family of God.

Ephesians 3 says to make every effort to keep the unity of the Spirit through the bond of peace. This is possible because there is one body, one Spirit, one hope, one Lord, one faith, one baptism, and one God the Father. Look at the heft you have in common! You focus on your differences, but look at the strength of your bond.

One body means the worldwide church of many members forming the legs and arms, eyes and ears of Christ on the earth. The body of Christ is united under Christ, who is the head. The body of Christ is the bride of Christ, who is the perfect complement to Christ the groom. Jesus said the body will do even greater works than he.

One Spirit means the same Spirit is poured out on all of you in order to counsel, protect, inspire, empower, and guide you. The goal of the Spirit is to glorify Jesus. The Spirit allots portions of grace to each of you so you fulfill what God assigned you to do.

One hope means you are assured of heaven because you are in Christ. This world and this body will fade away, dissolve, and fall apart, but this world is not the end. You were made for a better place, and you will spend eternity with God. Nothing anyone could do to you on earth can cancel your plans in eternity.

One Lord means that Christ came for you and forgave you, and on the basis of his shed blood on the cross, he conquered death for you. There is one way to heaven, and that is through Jesus. If there was not one way, not one Lord, but many ways, many lords, then Jesus' death was in vain and he didn't have to suffer so.

One faith means holding to the core beliefs of Christianity, although peripheral beliefs might disagree. You agree to the basics and don't let the extras interfere with your unity. You have different expressions of the same faith, different symbols, different rituals, but they don't divide you because you agree on the core.

One baptism means you have died to your old life and have been risen to your new life. You have announced that your allegiance is to the Father, Son, and Holy Spirit. You are a testimony to God's grace and are being transformed as you walk with God.

One God means you have been drawn to God's heart by God himself rather than a tyrant god, aloof god, powerless god, or sugar daddy god. You are loved by Father God. You have captured his heart so much that he sent his only son to die for you. He wants you to experience his Father heart. If you're in God's family, you have the same Father.

You have so much in common! This is why you can come

together in prayer despite your differences. When you decide to walk in peace together and keep short accounts, your one faith overwhelms the walls that try to separate, and you can then pray in agreement.

When the first two levels are in place, you can reach the third level of alignment—*the individual believer who is aligned with heaven joins other believers who are also aligned with heaven, and through the bond of peace, they agree on what heaven is saying.* This is agreement prayer.

Unfortunately, the church doesn't understand the power of agreement, and because of that, she doesn't walk in it. But agreement brings heaven to earth. Agreement unleashes the movement of God. Agreement was the key to the Acts church. It is possible to partner with God in such a manner that is more significant, more fruitful, and more explosive than in the book of Acts, but it will require the church operating in the prayer of agreement.

Here's what we must understand:

» God gave the earth to man to rule it. In Genesis 1, God commanded man to increase on the earth and subdue it. He said to rule over its inhabitants and work the land. Thus, the earth belongs to man because God gave it to him.

» Two or more witnesses create a quorum. A quorum is the number of people it takes to legally transact business. In the Bible, two or more witnesses established a matter. Jesus commissioned his disciples to go out two by two. A quorum formed a majority.

» When multiple believers agree in prayer, they form a spiritual majority that is capable of conducting legal transactions. As representatives of the earth, they stand in a place of authority regarding matters on earth. They pray from a heavenly position, but at the same time, they also pray from the earth.

For these reasons, God is looking for believers who will align with heaven to form a spiritual majority and transact business to impact the natural. This is why the prayer of agreement is so vital to God's kingdom on the earth. Agreement prayer opens up the heavens and establishes heaven on the earth.

Your friend calls back the next day. He wants to share the results of your agreement prayer.

"When we prayed, it transformed the whole way I was looking at it," he said.

He went in feeling defensive, like he was shrinking back. He felt apologetic for his purpose, questioned why he was there. He felt defeated even before he started.

But the prayer of agreement altered his perspective. He saw what God was up to, and along with you, he agreed with God's purposes. Who better than a Christian to bring light into darkness? Had another coworker gone, the light wouldn't have gone. But sometimes light just needs the chance to shine.

As brothers, you agreed with God so God's work could be established. That was the real work that night. Amen.

Tweets from this Chapter

> »   In the Bible, amen said by God is a word of establishment, while amen said by man is a word of agreement. @CSHeinz

> »   The book of Acts is the book of agreement prayer. All the time, the believers were praying together. @CSHeinz

> »   In order to achieve such tremendous growth and perform such amazing miracles, the Acts church knew how to align with heaven. @CSHeinz

» For Christians, the issue is not doing more to get to heaven, but becoming more aware of the heavenly position you have already. @CSHeinz

» What you have in common with other believers is stronger than your differences. Agreement is a special force of the family of God. @CSHeinz

» God is looking for believers who will align with heaven to form a spiritual majority and transact business to impact the natural. @CSHeinz

» Agreement prayer opens up the heavens and establishes heaven on the earth. @CSHeinz

Discussion Questions

1. What is the definition of the prayer of agreement?
2. What is the first level of alignment?
3. What does it mean that you are seated with Christ in heavenly places?
4. What is the second level of alignment?
5. Are there any people with whom you need to reconcile?
6. What are at least three things that all believers have in common?
7. What is the third level of alignment?
8. What is a quorum?
9. Why is God looking for believers who will agree with heaven?
10. Do you feel drawn to this prayer type?

Conclusion

The will of the one who sent us is that we be the one
who was sent. What we do is meant to be lived out of the
context of discovering and becoming the person we are.
—Robert Benson,
Between the Dreaming and the Coming True[25]

The thief comes to steal and kill and destroy; I have
come that they may have life, and have it to the full.
—John 10:10

L ET'S SAY YOU HAD A particular nightmare as a kid. It plagued
your childhood, and although it was always the same, it
continued to shock you the way the starting pistol rings in your
ear when you're not ready for it or when a very young person dies.
It was the last thing you expected to happen in your front yard.
You were five years old.

On that bright morning, there wasn't a cloud in the sky.
The lawn was green and freshly cut. The sun dripped light into
the kitchen window, which faced outward into the front yard.
Like other mornings, Mama washed dishes in the sink while she
watched you play. From her perch, she stood and scrubbed while

you played with toy cars, sunbeams twinkling off their shiny enamel, which matched the shiny, happy feeling you had.

You loved Mama, this strong and beautiful woman. Although she stood inside the house, you could feel her smooth arms around you outside. You felt safe. You could be a kid.

But suddenly a man came from nowhere and grabbed you. His rough, steel arms squeezed you tight. You dropped your fire engine. Its wheels spun as it plunked on the ground.

You looked at Mama, who would rescue you. But she was looking down at something in the sink—a piece of silverware, a dirty plate. Look up, Mama! You have to look up, please! Mama, look up, this is what I need! But she didn't look up.

So you opened your mouth to cry out. This would get her attention. But as you did, nothing came out. There wasn't a sound. Your voice was gone. The man cupped his hand over your mouth as you tried to yell again. Your hot breath filled his palm as your breath returned to you with the stench of sweat and smoke. But how dreadful, no sound came out!

As the strong man carried you away, your yard got smaller, and you got farther away from Mama, until finally your home disappeared. The wheels on your engine fell silent.

"The thief comes only to steal and kill and destroy," Jesus said.

You were made to pray, but the enemy has tried to steal your voice. You're afraid that your voice isn't powerful or important. You have not cultivated the voice placed in you from the beginning. But the truth is, your voice in prayer is far more powerful and important than you know.

The world doesn't encourage you to use it. The world wants you to comply with her ways. It's fast-paced, shallow, never stopping. It's pushing you to get ahead, to climb the ladder heading to nowhere. The culture doesn't want you to pray. Prayer is for the weak, the self-centered, the wallflowers, the paranoid. Prayer is the foolish magic of the uncivilized and the unenlightened, the world will say.

And your old nature pokes, "Why pray?" It would love to jump in with the world, please the old nature's comforts. It would love to be the voice that is speaking rather than submit to the voice that matters. Your old nature doesn't like prayer.

But if you listen, you will hear the voice that trumps them all, saying, "I have come to redeem your voice!" The enemy comes to steal, kill, and destroy, but God comes to restore what the enemy has taken. God is restoring your voice in prayer to what it was in the beginning. You were made to pray in freedom and authority.

When God restores your voice in prayer, he restores your walk with him. Prayer is your primary connection with God. Prayer is where God most fully experiences who you are. There are no games, no masks, no trickeries—it's just you and God.

You're naked before him with no chance of covering up. Prayer is your heart laid bare before God. But it's also where you most fully experience him, where God brings himself to be known by you. Your prayer life is the reflection of your walk with God. Restored prayer brings a restored relationship with him.

When God restores your prayer life, he also restores your image of yourself. At one time, you saw yourself and the things that happened to you in a certain way. But in prayer, God shows you his perspective. He helps you interpret what happened by revisiting your experiences with you.

God was there when your father beat you or when your friends betrayed you or during your life's greatest pains. These pains enforced certain beliefs about yourself, and no matter how justifiable they seemed, they are not God's thoughts about you. God doesn't rewrite the past, but he corrects your interpretation of it. Restored prayer creates a restored image of yourself.

A restored prayer life also restores your relationship with others. In the Bible, God says if you're preparing to come before him and realize you have something against your neighbor or your neighbor has something against you, first be reconciled to your neighbor. Then you can come back to your time with God.

The Bible also says to forgive others or else God won't forgive you. In prayer, God can change your heart for your neighbor or even more, your in-laws. That's because your prayer life is not just about you and God, it's also about others. Restored prayer causes restored relationships with others.

Prayer also restores the world to God. The cross is vertical, but it's also horizontal. Your prayer life is your greatest means of changing the world. When you find your voice in prayer, you begin loving others into the kingdom because in prayer you discover how to love them.

Your neighbors across the street might have parties into the wee hours of morning, which wake your children, and soon the whole house is up at 3:00 a.m. And you want to retaliate because you deserve to. But in prayer, God shows you how to love them instead of retaliating because he loves them too. Restored prayer restores the world to God.

Jesus says, "The thief comes to steal and kill and destroy; I have come that they may have life, and have it to the full" (John 10:10). Your restored prayer life is the most tangible expression of God's abundant life in you.

Now that you've read this book, keep a few things in mind. *First, finding your best prayer types is a journey.* Hopefully you took the prayer assessment, got the results, and compared them to what you learned in the book. An additional step was sharing the experience with your prayer partner, prayer community, or small group. Identifying your best prayer types is not done in three easy steps. You will have found your best prayer types when over time your prayer life becomes enjoyable, effective, and enduring as a result of praying those types. This is sensational prayer, and it's not discovered overnight.

Second, your best prayer types might change over time. Your prayer life is forever, so take a long-term approach. The fact that God made you to pray is unchanging, but your best ways to connect with him are not. What satisfied you in prior years might not satisfy you in later years. God might do something in your life, like give the gift of prophecy, which now enables you to consistently pray prophetic prayer whereas before you could not. Be open to how your best prayer types might change as you change.

Third, specific seasons of life might require different types of prayer. You might be drawn into seasons in which particular types of prayer seem more appropriate than others. For instance, let's say you started a weekend MBA program. Every other weekend you attend classes and in between you complete assignments. But you also have a family and a full-time job.

One night on a business trip, the anxiety hits you. You spend the entire night hunched over the toilet like a college freshman. Inebriated by worry with pressure seeping into your bloodstream, you can't hold your drink, so to say. But you remember you can pray the Bible. It's not the regular way you pray, but you can't form your own thoughts now. Your mind is weary.

So you grab the Bible from the drawer, turn to Psalm 1, and begin praying. As you do, the words begin to fill themselves in. At first, they're black words on a white page, but then they take on shape and meaning as you pray them. You see yourself as a lush, fertile tree with fruit growing from the branches and fresh leaves sprouting from them. You're planted next to nourishing water.

You realize that the Word of God is feeding you. Success will not come by your own ability, ingenuity or might, but only by the Lord. As a result, you sober up and find peace. And throughout your MBA program, when you're juggling work and school and family, you pray the Bible so it renews your tired and weary mind, even though it's not the regular way you pray.

Fourth, being able to practice all the prayer types enables you to respond effectively to any situation. This is called situational prayer. While seasonal prayer responds to the season of life that you're in, situational prayer responds to the immediate situation. Seasons can be long, but situations are temporary. Wisdom is the appropriate application of knowledge. When you're knowledgeable in all the prayer types, you'll become wise in the practice of prayer.

Applying each prayer type to the same situation yields different results. For example:

- » Agreement diffuses arguments
- » Confession acknowledges sin
- » Fellowship celebrates God's friendship
- » Intercession receives direction from God
- » Listening humbles you before God
- » Petition asks for God's help
- » Praise focuses on who God is
- » Praying the Bible renews the mind
- » Tongues affirm heavenly citizenship
- » Prophetic prayer delivers God's message
- » Thanksgiving creates peace
- » Warfare battles with the enemy

What result would you or God like to see? Don't focus your prayers on the problem. Instead focus your prayers on the answer. Pray the solution, not the problem. Ask God what type of prayer to pray. If you don't hear an answer, choose one you think delivers the result that is needed.

In order to develop in the prayer types, you can plan personal prayer retreats either at home or somewhere else. Since there are twelve prayer types discussed in this book, plan your time around the number twelve:

» Twelve-hour prayer retreat: Pray each prayer type for an hour for twelve hours total. This enables you to cover all twelve types in the course of a day. Or if you have less time, pray for thirty minutes of each prayer type for six hours total.

» Twelve-day prayer retreat: Spend time each day praying a different prayer type for twelve days total. This enables you to spend more time each day praying so you can work it into your regular routine. Praying every day for twelve days forms prayer into a daily habit.

» Thirty-day prayer retreat: Pray twelve days in a row of a different prayer type each day, then three days of your choice, then repeat the twelve days, then three days of your choice. This allows you to have multiple days of praying each prayer type along with the types that you choose.

» Twelve-month prayer retreat: To have an entire year of the twelve prayer types, focus on one prayer type for an entire month. You'll find yourself praying other ways according to the situation, but in this prayer retreat, you make focused time during the month to pray the prayer type of the month. After your year, you'll have an awesome understanding of the richness of prayer.

You can activate most of the prayer types whenever you want to. You can praise or offer thanksgiving or confess anytime. Even listening prayer—listening for God regardless of his speaking or not—is initiated by you because the key is positioning yourself to listen. But three of the prayer types depend on God's initiation. They are prophetic prayer, intercession, and tongues.

In prophetic prayer, God gives you a message to deliver to someone else. Unless God speaks the message to you, you don't have one to deliver. During your prayer time, if you want to pray prophetically, you can ask God if he wants to pass a message through you. If you don't hear anything, you can begin reading the Bible. The Bible is, after all, God's Word. The Bible is written prophecy, spoken from God to his scribes years ago. You might find that as you read the Bible, God leads you to give certain verses to certain people. This is a form of prophetic prayer.

In your desire to try prophetic prayer, guard yourself against having to produce a result. Make your desire known to God that you are available, and then leave it at the altar of prayer. If your goal is to come away with a word, you put yourself at greater risk of manufacturing a word yourself or receiving a demonic word. The purpose is to hear a pure word from God should he speak, and if he doesn't, to be okay with it.

If God doesn't speak one time in prayer, go back a second time. The Bible says to eagerly desire to prophesy. Eagerly desire doesn't mean you try once and give up. Recognizing God's voice takes time and practice, and the only way you grow is to try to hear God's voice.

Intercession is another type of prayer that is initiated by God. Intercession is God-led prayer. In petition prayer, you see a need and pray for it, but in intercession, God leads you to pray for a need. This happens in two ways. Either God draws you to pray for a need that you are not presently aware of, or you are aware of a need, but God leads you to pray for specific things about that need that you weren't aware of.

If you want to intercede, you can simply ask God if there's anything he wants you to intercede for, then wait to see what happens. Or you can begin with petition prayer by praying for needs that you are aware of, and then ask God if there's anything else to pray for within that need.

The third type of prayer that depends on God is praying in tongues. This is a spiritual gift that God gives to whom he wills. You can't pray in tongues unless God gives it to you. However, once you have it, you can pray in tongues whenever and wherever you want to. You're not dependent on God doing anything more.

If you want to pray in tongues, ask God for the gift. Until then, treat tongues like spiritual poetry. If you're doing a prayer retreat and it's time for tongues, pray in such a manner you do not usually pray. Poets write poetry in order to express truths that transcend regular prose. Tongues function like that—expressing truths that transcend human language. So pray to God in poetry.

Fifth, corporate prayer is empowered by a variety of prayer types. Imagine identifying the spiritual stronghold of a city, say loneliness or poverty. According to Ed Silvoso, a spiritual stronghold is "a mind-set impregnated with hopelessness that causes us to accept as unchangeable, situations that we know are contrary to the Will of God."[26] Strongholds are spiritual in origin but have natural consequences. A stronghold of loneliness might cause binge drinking or sexual promiscuity, for example.

When individual pray-ers in a city learn their best prayer types and begin to practice them with authority, they grow in their walk with God. Not only that, but they begin to talk with God about their neighbors and begin walking through open doors to minister to them. But not only that, when people join prayers for the city, they confront strongholds with great force and agreement and reestablish the city on God.

People from all over the city come together, praying in their voices. There are thanksgiving pray-ers and warfare pray-ers and intercessors. The Bible is prayed and so is praise and also confession, all united in agreement prayer. This is a true concert of prayer!

Before they learned their prayer types, they never saw themselves as city pray-ers. They were living their solitary lives in boredom and frustration, wanting to be part of something more but not knowing how or what. But now they take their place in bringing God's kingdom to the city. And when the city is changed, the nation can be changed and the ends of the earth. How does this happen? By one prayer at a time, and one person at a time.

"Let's go up the mountain," you announce to your family. And when you say that, your family knows what you mean. Your children grab their worship flags, and your wife grabs her Bible. This won't be an ordinary hike. The mountain overlooks the valley and is the highest place in the land. You're going to do business on the mountain.

You don't have the nightmare anymore. There's no strongman carrying you away. You have found your voice. Your prayer life is full of strength and power.

You park in the gravel lot and begin to climb. You take turns waving the flags up the mountain. Together you declare the promises of God along the trail. You praise the Lord with shouts and claps, blow the shofar once in a while. And from the top of the mountain, the highest land around, you pray the prayers on your heart. Prayers to strengthen your walk with God. Prayers to reach your neighbors. Prayers to establish the city of God.

As you look across the valley, you see homes and businesses and schools. You see bars and streets and stadiums. You see cars on the highway and planes in the sky. You wonder how many people out there are locked up, silent, needing something more. They sit quietly in the pews, have given up on reaching their neighbors, simply work their jobs and go home to television. They don't go beyond their own lives and their families.

But you see something more in the valley.

You see the people of God, full of the elements God put in them when they were made in the beginning. They are a spiritual house, a royal priesthood. They are on this earth but belong to heaven. You see prayers on their hearts, waiting to be prayed. You see angels at attention, waiting to be dispatched. You see miracles on hold, waiting to be performed. They're all across the valley, just waiting to be released. Waiting for the ones who were sent to become the ones they are.

The thief comes to steal and kill and destroy, but Jesus comes to bring abundant life.

Take up your voice, person of God. You were made to pray!

Tweets from this Conclusion

> » You were made to pray, but the enemy has tried to steal your voice. You're afraid that your voice isn't powerful or important. @CSHeinz

> » God doesn't rewrite the past, but he corrects your interpretation of it. @CSHeinz

> » When you find your voice in prayer, you begin loving others into the kingdom because in prayer you discover how to love them. @CSHeinz

> » Specific seasons of life might require different types of prayer. @CSHeinz

> » Being able to practice all the prayer types enables you to respond effectively to any situation. @CSHeinz

> » Don't focus your prayers on the problem. Instead focus

your prayers on the answer. Pray the solution, not the problem. @CSHeinz

» When people join prayers for the city, they confront strongholds with great force and agreement and re-establish the city on God. @CSHeinz

» The thief comes to steal and kill and destroy, but Jesus comes to bring abundant life. Take up your voice, person of God! @CSHeinz

Discussion Questions

1. How did you feel as you read about the nightmare?
2. Has your voice been silenced? How?
3. When your prayer life gets restored, what three areas get restored?
4. What does it mean that God doesn't rewrite the past, but corrects your interpretation of it?
5. What is sensational prayer? What is seasonal prayer? What is situational prayer?
6. What three prayer types require initiation by God?
7. Have you ever thought of yourself as a city pray-er? Do you now?
8. Can you identify any spiritual strongholds in your city? How are they impacting your city?
9. What godly principles do you want to establish in your city?
10. If you could choose three prayer types for a prayer retreat, what would they be?

Prayer Assessment

About the Assessment

Also available at www.MadeToPray.com, the assessment is a series of statements about your prayer life. You'll read each statement, then select an answer that most closely relates. After 60 statements, you'll have the option of stopping or going on. If you stop, you can score your assessment. If you go on, you'll complete 60 more statements, then score your results. The 60-statement version takes less time, but the longer one might be more accurate.

Please keep in mind this is not a scientific assessment. While it has been tested for usability, clarity, and accuracy of results, the assessment is not hard science. It's meant to assist you in finding the types of prayer that work best for you. The assessment is intended to be used alongside the book.

Taking the Assessment

Fill in the white box with the choice that most closely relates to the statement about your prayer life. Don't answer as you wish things were; answer as things currently are.

For example:

I'm okay with asking God for the same things over and over again.

> » Don't Identify At All...............this is never true for you
> » Seldom or Mostly Do Not Identify....this is mostly never true for you
> » Sometimes or Partially Identify...........this is sometimes true for you
> » Usually or Mostly Identify.........this is usually true for you
> » Always Identify.....................this is always true for you

After you complete the assessment, score your results by adding the white boxes and entering the subtotal for each column on each page. The maximum score for each prayer type is 120 points for the longer version and 60 points for the shorter one.

After the Assessment

After taking the assessment, read the book to compare your results with the chapters. The assessment is not intended to do apart from the book. For the best experience, we recommend you: 1) do the assessment; 2) read the book; and 3) share the experience with your community. Your community might consist of your prayer partner, mentor, parent, small group or Bible study group. You can find your best prayer types together.

Don't Identify At All	Seldom or Mostly Do Not Identify	Sometimes or Partially Identify	Usually or Mostly Identify	Always Identify
0	3	6	9	12

1	I'm okay with asking God for the same things over and over again.
2	I treat God more like a friend than the Holy God.
3	I am spiritually energized when I affirm who God is.
4	I can easily put myself in other people's situations.
5	I pray in tongues, which is my personal spiritual language.
6	I am more bold and confident when I'm praying than when I'm not praying.
7	I believe Jesus helps me do the work he has called me to do.
8	After acknowledging my sin, I naturally flow into praise.
9	Praying the Bible helps me understand the Bible better.
10	I need courage to share the messages God gives me for others.
11	I sense what to pray for without a person telling me.
12	God has revealed future events to me.
13	I understand the power of a thank you.
14	Sometimes I can't find the words to express what's on my heart.
15	When I pray alone, silence often seems more appropriate than speaking.

1-15 SUBTOTAL

16	When I read the Bible, it leads me to pray.
17	I frequently quiet my heart to receive from God.
18	People have misunderstood my time with God as laziness.
19	I pray in tongues as much as I pray in my human language.
20	I want people to hear from God.
21	I can use prayer as a tool to accomplish the work of God's kingdom.
22	I feel that God is patient with my prayer requests.
23	I like the idea of praying without ceasing.
24	I protect time in my schedule for activities that draw me closer to God.
25	I often think of Jesus as my intercessor because he stands in the gap for me.
26	I feel encouraged when I pray in tongues.
27	I'm content to listen to God even if he doesn't speak.
28	God has used me to set people free from things that were holding them back.
29	Community plays a big role in my faith.
30	I think that even insignificant things deserve to be prayed for.

16-30 SUBTOTAL

31	I really value putting God's word in my heart.															
32	I tend to think of my sins more as a sinful nature than as individual acts.															
33	It feels natural to involve God in the mundane parts of my day.															
34	I renew my mind by meditating on Scripture.															
35	I like to serve behind the scenes.															
36	Others have identified me as a wise person.															
37	I need Jesus to help me now as much as ever.															
38	I have asked angels for help.															
39	I'm torn up if I'm not at peace with everyone.															
40	I have received a message from God for someone else.															
41	I outwardly express my agreement when others are praying.															
42	I grow as a Christian when I pray the Bible.															
43	If I don't understand what I'm praying, I still trust that it holds meaning and power.															
44	It's natural for me to come to God with boldness.															
45	I easily notice small blessings that other people don't.															
31-45 SUBTOTAL																

46	While others may get weary, I could celebrate my salvation again and again.												▢		
47	When I pray, the first thing I do is confess my sins.												▢		
48	It's easy to believe in a world I cannot readily see.													▢	
49	I can perceive supernatural influences on people, places, and situations.													▢	
50	When I pray, I'm often convicted about relationships I need to make right.							▢							
51	I can proclaim God's goodness even when I don't feel like it.				▢										
52	I'm saddened when I see broken relationships.						▢								
53	I'm excited that God is everywhere.									▢					
54	I'm not easily stressed.	▢													
55	Sharing a message from God is one of my greatest ways to serve.					▢									
56	I celebrate God's character traits.						▢								
57	God's character should be relished.					▢									
58	I begin my prayers by thanking God.	▢													
59	I'm an optimistic person.	▢													
60	It's easy to remember what God has done for me.						▢								

46-60 SUBTOTAL

Congratulations! You've finished 60 statements. If you would like to end here, go to *Scoring Your Assessment*. To continue the assessment, keep going.

61	God has spoken to me directly.
62	The thought of a heavenly language excites me.
63	I can easily find things to pray for.
64	I understand the people of God not only as a family, but also as an army.
65	I like being silent before God.
66	Justice for the helpless is important to me.
67	I try to live in the moment.
68	I am conscious of evil more often than others seem to be.
69	It makes me sad to think about my sinfulness.
70	When I pray, Scripture often comes to mind.
71	I help others see what God has done for them.
72	I would like God's people to be united.
73	To focus on God rather than myself, I use Scripture in prayer.
74	My faith is strengthened when I pray in my spirit language.
75	There are certain non-religious activities that help me feel the presence of God.

61-75 SUBTOTAL

76	I gladly spend long periods of time alone with God.													
77	I like to clear my mind and fill it with God.													
78	Being with God is better than God doing anything for me.													
79	Thanking God is more important to me than asking for things.													
80	I feel dependent on the peace of God to guard my heart and mind.													
81	Unforgiveness is one of the biggest problems.													
82	My prayers seem to be answered more often than other people's.													
83	I am in constant awe of God's forgiveness.													
84	I have changed the spiritual climate of a room by praising God.													
85	I love to focus on the wonderful attributes of God.													
86	I have felt power when praying with a group of people.													
87	I often pray on the spot when there's a need.													
88	I want everyone to hear God's message for him or her.													
89	I'm content appearing undignified when I pray.													
90	When I've done something wrong, I can move past guilt easily.													

76-90 SUBTOTAL

91	I am content with little.	
92	I wait for God to direct my prayers.	
93	I get so much out of praying in tongues that I want others to pray in tongues, too.	
94	I like to pray with other people.	
95	I have a heightened sense of the Holy Spirit when I read the 3.	
96	I could go on and on about the greatness of God.	
97	I believe that God uses my prayers to change things.	
98	I get nervous about praying for something that isn't God's will.	
99	God is on my mind all the time.	
100	I grow in my relationship with God beyond religious activities.	
101	I appreciate the different perspective people bring in prayer.	
102	I see myself as a participant in the cosmic battle of good and evil.	
103	It's easy for me to believe in the supernatural world.	
104	I'm comfortable asking God for things.	
105	When I read the Bible, I connect it with my life.	
91-105 SUBTOTAL		

106	Giving thanks energizes me.
107	Intimacy with God is more important than answered prayers.
108	I love that God communicates with people.
109	There are certain activities in which I feel closer to God.
110	When I can't think of what to pray, I let my spirit pray.
111	I feel comfortable talking casually with God.
112	I am often reminded of the suffering Jesus endured for my salvation.
113	I try to be humble when delivering from God.
114	I press through distractions to listen to God.
115	I enjoy encouraging people with my words.
116	I have sensed an evil presence before.
117	I understand that when I do wrong, it emphasizes God's perfect character.
118	I like to partner with God in speaking his word to others.
119	I like to express my love for God in a variety of ways.
120	I go to special places to spend time with God.

106-120 SUBTOTAL

Scoring Your Assessment

Add the points in each column on every page.

Transfer the subtotals to this grid and add the points from each page.

	1	2	3	4	5	6	7	8	9	10	11	12
1-15 SUBTOTAL												
16-30 SUBTOTAL												
31-45 SUBTOTAL												
46-60 SUBTOTAL												
61-75 SUBTOTAL												
76-90 SUBTOTAL												
91-105 SUBTOTAL												
105-120 SUBTOTAL												
TOTAL												

Transfer the total numbers for each prayer type; these are your scores.

1		Thanksgiving Prayer
2		Petition Prayer
3		Praying the Bible
4		Listening Prayer
5		Prophetic Prayer
6		Praise
7		Praying in Tongues
8		Agreement Prayer
9		Fellowship Prayer
10		Confession
11		Warfare Prayer
12		Intercession

Prayer Type Chart

Symbol	Prayer Type	Definition	Character	Verse
	Agreement	Multiple believers agreeing on earth with what heaven is saying	Acts church	Matthew 18:19–20
	Confession	Acknowledging your sin to God, and then celebrating the forgiveness you have received	David (2 Samuel 11–12)	Psalm 51:2–3
	Fellowship	Spending time with God in an activity that is not traditionally sacred or prayerful	Adam and Eve	Genesis 3:8
	Intercession	God leading you to pray for the needs of a person, place, or cause	Anna	Luke 2:37
	Listening	Sitting at the feet of Jesus and listening for him	Mary of Bethany (Luke 10:38–42)	Psalm 46:10

Symbol	Prayer Type	Definition	Character	Verse
	Petition	Seeing a need and praying for it	The Leper and the Centurion (Matthew 8:2–10)	Luke 11:9
	Praise	Declaring the truth about who God is, what he has done, or what he has promised to do	Peter	Psalm 150:6
	Praying the Bible	Praying the words of the Bible as your prayer	Joshua	Joshua 1:8
	Tongues	Praying in a personal spiritual language that edifies you and your relationship with God	Paul	1 Corinthians 14:14
	Prophetic	Receiving a message from God for someone else	Jeremiah	Jeremiah 1:7
	Thanksgiving	Offering thanks to God	Paul	1 Thessalonians 5:18
	Warfare	Confronting the kingdom of Satan with the weapons of God's kingdom	The Seventy-two Others (Luke 10:1–20)	Ephesians 6:12

103 Tweets from *Made to Pray*

If you want to encourage others in their prayer lives through Twitter, Facebook or other ways, here are 103 short inspirational quotations from *Made to Pray*:

Introduction

» When you pray, God gets something no one else can give him—God gets you. @CSHeinz

» Prayer is where God pours out his love every day. Prayer is where God loves you. @CSHeinz

» Prayer is the reward of walking with God, but so often we treat it like punishment. @CSHeinz

» When prayer is as it can be, it will not matter where you live, or what you wear, or what you eat because prayer will sustain you. @CSHeinz

» Finding your best prayer types frees you and others up to uniquely connect with God. @CSHeinz

» When you find your sweet spot in prayer, you can have prayer that's enjoyable, effective and enduring—prayer as it's meant to be. @CSHeinz

» Your prayer life is your greatest means of changing the world for Christ. @CSHeinz

» When you pray, you can receive strategies for reaching your neighbors, and by reaching your neighbors, you reach the world. @CSHeinz

Prayer of Praise

» When you limit praise to music, you perfect the music, but forget the point. Praise is about God, his deeds, and his promises. @CSHeinz

» Your heart abandoned to God—and not perfect music—is the root of real worship. God prefers passion over form. @CSHeinz

» God is at work more than you know. What you need is not for God to do more, but for you to see more of what God has already done. @CSHeinz

» God is looking for people who will stand on his promises regardless of what they do not see. This is living by faith. @CSHeinz

» Praise is meant to be a sacrifice and is one of the only things you offer God that is truly your own. It is borne of your freedom. @CSHeinz

» If you want God's glory, then praise him. He visits altars established to him and answers sacrifices offered to him. @CSHeinz

» A strategy of the enemy in worship is to shift the focus from God to you. You'll think you deserve to be comfortable in praise. @CSHeinz

» When God does something for you, share it! Your

testimony is a seed of praise that spurs faith in others when they don't have any. @CSHeinz

» When things go wrong, they take control. But in reality, God's still on the throne. Praise puts things in the right perspective. @CSHeinz

Petition Prayer

» A secret to asking God for something is to just do it. You don't get if you don't ask. @CSHeinz

» A problem in prayer is asking for what you already have, what you can do on your own, or what you already see. This isn't faith. @CSHeinz

» God won't slap you when you draw near. He'll pull you into his strong, loving arms, which are iron and velvet at once. @CSHeinz

» Learn to ask for what you want God to do, but submit to his will when you do. @CSHeinz

» Sometimes felt needs are doors into people's hearts where the Father can meet them. @CSHeinz

» The goal of praying for people is an encounter with God. When this becomes your goal, then praying for people is suddenly doable. @CSHeinz

» When God shows up, help the person understand what happened. Interpret for them. This is how you preach the gospel through prayer. @CSHeinz

» Failure to risk occurs most often because you didn't take the first step. @CSHeinz

Intercessory Prayer

» In petition prayer, you see a need and pray for it, but in intercession, God shows you the need so you can pray for it. @CSHeinz

» Intercession is marked by three qualities: intimacy, guidance, and identification. @CSHeinz

» The intercessor loves God and knows his face. She spends long and deep periods of time with him and has the key to his house. @CSHeinz

» Incarnation and habitation are different. Jesus incarnated because of sin, but the Holy Spirit habitates because of obedience. @CSHeinz

» In intercession, God doesn't always send a vision or word. Sometimes he sends a burden that is like labor unto birth. So birth it! @CSHeinz

» You can't get to God on your own, not by hours on the treadmill or feeding hungry children or lifelong learning. By Christ alone. @CSHeinz

» Sometimes you find ways to identify for whom you intercede, but other times God helps you identify with them. @CSHeinz

Prophetic Prayer

» God's Word will work on you, even against your steel will and crossed arms. The soul made by God and for God is being affected. @CSHeinz

» An alarming thing about God is his full access. Not only does he have the nerve to interfere with your life, he can do it anytime. @CSHeinz

» God could get on a loud speaker, draw in sand, speak through your dachshund. But sometimes God uses messengers to deliver his word. @CSHeinz

» When God speaks, you're reminded that he cares for you. This word can reassemble the world as you know it. @CSHeinz

» God uses prophecy when he has more to say than is in the Bible. When the Bible was canonized in 1546, God didn't stop talking. @CSHeinz

» God uses prophecy to benefit the common good, which is the church and the world. Prophecy can open the heart of an unbeliever. @CSHeinz

» Prophecy can function in three ways: as a spiritual gift, as an anointing, and as an office. @CSHeinz

Listening Prayer

» Mary and Martha teach us that when Jesus is present, it's better to be a guest than a host. @CSHeinz

» Listening prayer is being silent so that God becomes your only noise. It's to be still and know that he is God (Psalm 46:10). @CSHeinz

» Listening prayer is quieting yourself to the hush of the Almighty so your soul is satisfied in him. You feast in his presence. @CSHeinz

» When anything trumps your devotion to Jesus, it's fair game to be removed. Nothing is more sacred. @CSHeinz

» The one who listens for God has trained her heart to be satisfied in him. It is then that she can be trusted with ministry. @CSHeinz

» Jesus would rather you sit with him than serve him. He is more jealous for your presence than he is for your service. @CSHeinz

» The measure of your love for God should make your other devotions seem like hate. @CSHeinz

» Listening prayer is hard because it requires you to strip off attachments and let go of performances and just be with God. @CSHeinz

Fellowship Prayer

» God's not always loud. Sometimes he whispers loud enough to recognize, maybe a butterfly crowning, a breeze blowing, a baby cooing. @CSHeinz

» Growth is like a garden. Sometimes God turns the soil or waters or weeds, but it's always good. Gardens teach you seasons of life. @CSHeinz

» Judgment for sin demanded a perfect man in return. God could not be exchanged for man's sin; a perfect man had to stand in the gap. @CSHeinz

» A friend of God knows what God sounds like, soft or loud. And he goes out to meet him, wherever it is. @CSHeinz

» Fellowship prayer is spending time with God in an activity that is not traditionally sacred or prayerful. @CSHeinz

Warfare Prayer

» You were born into the conflict between God and Satan. The conflict is spiritual, but it manifests on the earth. @CSHeinz

» God wants you to follow him so you'll have abundant life. Satan doesn't. Like all wars it's a matter of life and death. @CSHeinz

» The term "Christian" means follower of Christ. The purpose of Christianity is to produce people who follow Christ. @CSHeinz

» Satan is a loser because well, he lost. Jesus disarmed the powers and authorities and made a public spectacle of them (Col 2:15). @CSHeinz

» Sometimes the Holy Spirit leads you into battle to overcome the enemy. He isn't safe or interested in keeping you comfortable. @CSHeinz

» The blood of Jesus is the most powerful substance in the universe because it liberates you from death when you receive it. @CSHeinz

» One underutilized weapon in God's kingdom is your accessibility to angels, but you can ask God to send angels to help you. @CSHeinz

» In fasting, you go without your natural comforts, fall-backs, and routines, so God becomes your one and only. @CSHeinz

» Forgiveness is a supernatural act that closes the door to demonic entry. @CSHeinz

Praying the Bible

» Praying the Bible is praying the words of the Bible as your prayer. @CSHeinz

» Meditating on God's Word is not an emptying, but a filling of the timeless wisdom of God. When you meditate on God, you are filled. @CSHeinz

» When you pray the Bible, you join in an activity practiced by generations before you. It connects you to your roots. @CSHeinz

» Here are four ways to pray the Bible: meditating on it, making it personal, mashing up Bible prayers, and moving through a list. @CSHeinz

» If you want to know God's will, then get to know God's word, and if you want to pray God's will, then pray God's Word. @CSHeinz

» Praying the Bible fixes your mind on God. The mind can be a hapless organ. You tell it what to do, but it doesn't listen. @CSHeinz

» When you pray the Bible, you grip the sword that divides soul and spirit. @CSHeinz

Prayer of Confession

» You'd rather flaunt your good deeds than finger your sin, but all the while your sin is stinking up the place. @CSHeinz

» Not all nice people go to heaven. If you've sinned once, you've sinned a million times. @CSHeinz

» For confession of sin to be Christian, forgiveness must be received on account of Christ. This wells up in great celebration. @CSHeinz

» God has a way of exposing sin in order to foster repentance. He's more into your growth and goodness than you are. @CSHeinz

» Only when you look at yourself honestly and claim what is true can the power of confession begin to work. You have to own your sin. @CSHeinz

» Confession draws you out, the one who was hiding. You find out what you've been doing is not who you really are. @CSHeinz

» Don't keep your sin alive. What Jesus calls dead, leave dead. @CSHeinz

Prayer of Thanksgiving

» Not only did the apostle Paul practice thanksgiving prayer in his personal faith, he encouraged others to do the same. @CSHeinz

» As a Christian, peace is your inheritance. An inheritance isn't given unless someone dies. Jesus died for your peace, so live it. @CSHeinz

» Pursue peace like it's your calling. Live in such a way that your life echoes your salvation. @CSHeinz

» Thanksgiving assures you that Jesus is enough. @CSHeinz

» Biblical thanksgiving is more of a choice than a feeling. @CSHeinz

» The value you place on thanksgiving, and really anything God says, is revealed in the tough times. @CSHeinz

» If you really believe in giving thanks at all times, then give thanks where it's hardest—at the Dung Gate. What's your Dung Gate? @CSHeinz

Praying in Tongues

» Sometimes human language isn't adequate to communicate with God. Praying in tongues is like spiritual poetry. @CSHeinz

» Praying in tongues helps you pray what is bigger than human words allow. Your relationship with God is the epic romance after all. @CSHeinz

» Your essence is not flesh, it's spirit. And God is not flesh, he's spirit. Praying in tongues is the language of the spirit. @CSHeinz

» The gift of tongues cannot add or detract from the fact of your salvation, but it can improve the experience of your salvation. @CSHeinz

» We know Paul the Missionary and Paul the Apostle, but do we know Paul the Tongues-Speaker? He spoke in tongues more than anyone. @CSHeinz

» Sometimes God withholds an answer to prayer in order to produce in us deeper holiness, discipleship, praise, or even desperation. @CSHeinz

Prayer of Agreement

» In the Bible, amen said by God is a word of establishment, while amen said by man is a word of agreement. @CSHeinz

» The book of Acts is the book of agreement prayer. All the time, the believers were praying together. @CSHeinz

» In order to achieve such tremendous growth and perform such amazing miracles, the Acts church knew how to align with heaven. @CSHeinz

» For Christians, the issue is not doing more to get to heaven, but becoming more aware of the heavenly position you have already. @CSHeinz

» What you have in common with other believers is stronger

than your differences. Agreement is a special force of the family of God. @CSHeinz

» God is looking for believers who will align with heaven to form a spiritual majority and transact business to impact the natural. @CSHeinz

» Agreement prayer opens up the heavens and establishes heaven on the earth. @CSHeinz

Conclusion

» You were made to pray, but the enemy has tried to steal your voice. You're afraid that your voice isn't powerful or important. @CSHeinz

» God doesn't rewrite the past, but he corrects your interpretation of it. @CSHeinz

» When you find your voice in prayer, you begin loving others into the kingdom because in prayer you discover how to love them. @CSHeinz

» Specific seasons of life might require different types of prayer. @CSHeinz

» Being able to practice all the prayer types enables you to respond effectively to any situation. @CSHeinz

» Don't focus your prayers on the problem. Instead focus your prayers on the answer. Pray the solution, not the problem. @CSHeinz

» When people join prayers for the city, they confront strongholds with great force and agreement and re-establish the city on God. @CSHeinz

» The thief comes to steal and kill and destroy, but Jesus comes to bring abundant life. Take up your voice, person of God! @CSHeinz

Sources

1. Benson, Robert. *In Constant Prayer.* Nashville: Thomas Nelson, 2008.

2. Foster, Richard. *Celebration of Discipline.* New York: HarperCollins, 1998.

3. Tirabassi, Becky. *Let Prayer Change Your Life – Revised.* Nashville: Thomas Nelson, 2001.

4. Foster, Richard. *Celebration of Discipline.* New York: HarperCollins, 1998.

5. "Hallow." *Vine's Complete Expository Dictionary of Old and New Testament Words.* Nashville: Thomas Nelson Publishers, 1996.

6. Buechner, Frederick. *Listening to Your Life.* New York: HarperSanFrancisco, 1992.

7. Bonhoeffer, Dietrich. *The Cost of Discipleship.* New York: Macmillan Publishing Company, 1963.

8. Dillard, Annie. "Write Till You Drop." *The New York Times on the Web,* May 28, 1989. http://www.nytimes. com/books/99/03/28/specials/dillard-drop.html

9. Bounds, E.M. *The Power of Prayer.* Bloomingdale, IL: Christian Art Gifts, 2007.

10. Grubb, Norman. *Rees Howells, Intercessor.* Fort Washington, PA: CLC Publications, 2008.

11. Ibid.

12. Ibid.

13. Storms, Sam. *The Beginner's Guide to Spiritual Gifts.* Ann Arbor, Servant Publications, 2002.

14. "Word." *Vine's Complete Expository Dictionary of Old and New Testament Words.* Nashville: Thomas Nelson Publishers, 1996.

15. Foster, Richard. *Celebration of Discipline.* New York: HarperSanFrancisco, 1988.

16. Pascal, Blaise. *Pensees.* Oxford: Benediction Classics, 2011.

17. Brother Lawrence. *The Practice of the Presence of God.* Grand Rapids, MI: Bake Publishing Group, 1967.

18. Silvoso, Ed. *That None Should Perish.* Ventura, CA: Regal Books, 1994.

19. Lewis, C.S. *The Lion, the Witch, and the Wardrobe.* New York: HarperCollins, 2000.

20. Wagner, C. Peter. *What the Bible Says About Spiritual Warfare.* Ventura, CA: Regal Books, 2002.

21. Kopp, David. *Praying the Bible for Your Life.* Colorado Springs: WaterBrook Press, 1999.

22. Vine, W.E. *Vine's Complete Expository Dictionary of Old and New Testament Words.* Nashville: Thomas Nelson Publishers, 1996.

23. Gresh, Dannah. *The Secret of the Lord.* Nashville: Thomas Nelson, 2005.

24. Voskamp, Ann. *One Thousand Gifts*. Grand Rapids, MI: Zondervan, 2010.

25. Isleib, Mary Alice. *Effective Fervent Prayer*. Rockford, IL: Mary Alice Isleib Ministries, 1991.

26. Alves, Beth. Becoming A Prayer Warrior. Ventura, CA: Regal Books, 1998.

27. Benson, Robert. *Between the Dreaming and the Coming True*. New York: Jeremy P. Tarcher/Putnam, 1996.

28. Silvoso, Ed. *That None Should Perish*. Ventura, CA: Regal Books, 1994.